Options in Contemporary Christian Ethics

Norman L. Geisler

D1561771

BAKER BOOK HOUSE

Grand Rapids, Michigan 49506

WARNER MEMORIAL LIBRARY
EASTERN UNIVERSITY
ST. DAVIDS, PA 19087-3696

BJ
1251
.G43

Copyright 1981 by
Baker Book House Company
ISBN: 0-8010-3757-3

First printing, February 1981
Second printing, February 1984

Library of Congress Catalog Card Number: 80-69431

Printed in the United States of America

Unless otherwise noted, all Scripture references are taken from The Revised
Standard Version, © 1946, 1952, 1971, 1973 by the Division of Christian Educa-
tion of the National Council of the Churches of Christ in the United States of
America.

Contents

101458

Introduction

Despite a strong emphasis on the moral aspect of biblical truth, evangelicals have not produced an abundance of books on ethics. And those produced are all too often more practical than principial, and they are usually more negative than positive. In this later regard we have been better at smelling rotten eggs than at laying good ones. We have rightly sensed the inadequacy of a purely situational ethic, but we have not always offered a better positive alternative.

There are many reasons for this failure, not the least of which is the lack of a systematic approach to the topic. It is all too common for contemporary evangelicals to share the current existential and pragmatic distaste for "systems," whether they are theological or ethical. We have often forsaken systematic theology for practical or relational theology and have considered systematic ethics to be little more than exhortations against "worldliness." Often we have treated isolated moral topics, but we seldom do so within a comprehensive and consistent ethical framework or system.

There have been three main ethical systems historically embraced by evangelicals. This book is an attempt to examine the merits and problems of each perspective. Thereby, we hope to bring into focus both the options available as well as some of the moral and theological implications of these various frameworks. Not the least of the benefits that may accrue to those who discover the hidden "system" of their own ethical convictions is that it will provide a helpful ethical base. From this base one can make important decisions on pressing contemporary ethical issues not explicitly addressed in Scripture (such as genetic control, artificial insemination, cloning, test-tube babies, and so forth).

The popular aversion to ethical "systems" and "theories" is ill-founded, as is evident from the words of a psychologist friend who once told me, "A good theory is a very *practical* thing." Likewise, it is my hope that evangelicals will come to realize that as we are faced with the exigencies of ethical decision-making in the twentieth century, a good (biblical, comprehensive, and consistent) ethical "system" is a very helpful thing.

Norman L. Geisler

No Option

Relativism

Christian ethics is firmly absolutist. It is based on the character of an unchanging God "who cannot lie" (Titus 1:2, NEB). It is manifest in God's law which "cannot be broken" (John 10:35, NIV) and in the person of Jesus Christ who "is the same yesterday, today and forever" (Heb. 13:8, NEB). Total relativism, therefore, is no option for a Christian. To be realistic, however, we must acknowledge that we live in a relativistic age. "Absolutism" is for most an archaic and untenable concept. Hence, it is necessary for us to understand the background for ethical relativism and respond to the arguments for this position.

Relativism: Arguments and Counter-Arguments

From ancient times men have been impressed with the flux and mobility of life. These observations led some to lay down premises that have been used to justify the belief that there are no absolutes. Translated into the ethical realm this would mean total moral relativity.

Relativism in the Ancient World

There are at least three movements in the ancient world which influenced ethical relativism: processism, hedonism, and skepticism.

Processism. Heraclitus said, "No man steps into the same river twice, for fresh waters are ever upon him."[1] Everything in the world is in a continual state of flux. Cratylus carried this flux philosophy even farther, concluding that no one could step into the same river even once. The river—and everything else—has no "sameness" or unchanging essence. So completely did Cratylus believe that all is flux that he was not even sure he existed. When asked about his existence, he would simply wiggle his finger, indicating that he too was in flux. It goes without saying that if this process philosophy is correct, then there are no unchanging absolutes, ethical or otherwise.

Two points can be made here in response to this position. First, it is important to note that Heraclitus was not a total relativist. He did believe that there was an unchanging *logos* beneath all change and by which the change itself is measured.[2] Indeed, Heraclitus believed that all men should live by this absolute law in the midst of the flux of life. Second, Cratylus carried the idea of change so far that it became self-contradicting. For when everything is changing and nothing is constant, then there is no way to know that things are changing. But when the idea of change is destroyed, one is back at the unchanging. Total change is a self-destructive concept. In short, everything cannot be in process.

---

1. See Heraclitus in Reginald E. Allen, ed., *Greek Philosophy: Thales to Aristotle* (New York: Macmillan, 1966), p. 42.
2. Allen, *Greek Philosophy*, p. 41.

Hedonism. The Epicureans gave impetus to a relativistic ethic by making pleasure the essence of good and pain the essence of evil.[3] But pleasures are relative to individuals and their tastes. A jet ride is pleasure for some, and sheer agony for others! If, then, the good is the pleasurable and yet pleasure is relative, then what is good is relative to the time and tastes of particular persons. According to this view, what is morally good for one may be evil for another and vice versa.

The objections to hedonism fall into several categories. First, not all pleasures are good. The sadistic pleasure some disturbed persons may receive from tormenting children is evil. Second, not all pain is bad. Pain which warns of impending disease or damage is a good pain. Further, it is a category mistake to confuse tastes and values. Tastes may be largely (or even entirely) relative, but basic values are not. Tastes are feelings persons *have* and vary depending on the circumstances. But values are what persons *are;* persons are still persons no matter how their circumstances change. Therefore, all values are not totally relative.

Skepticism. The central thesis of skepticism is: Suspend judgment on all truth claims.[4] The skeptic claims each issue has two sides, and all issues can be argued to a stalemate. Since we cannot come to any firm and final

---

3. Epicurus himself was not an "Epicurean." He lived a simple life without dietary excess. He did say, "We call pleasure the alpha and omega of a blessed life. Pleasure is our first and kindred good. It is the starting point of every choice and of every aversion." He added, however, "Oftimes we consider pain superior to pleasures when submission to the pains for a long time brings us as a consequence a greater pleasure." *Greek and Roman Philosophy After Aristotle,* ed. Jason Saunders (New York: Macmillan, 1966), p. 51.

4. Ancient skepticism was summed up in the writings of Sextus Empiricus. See Saunders, *Greek and Roman Philosophy,* pp. 152-82.

conclusions on anything, says the skeptic, the wise man simply doubts everything. He refuses to make any firm conclusions. In ethics, this would mean one should never consider anything as absolutely or universally right or wrong.

There are numerous problems with skepticism. First of all, the skeptic is at root dogmatic, for there is one thing on which he himself is not willing to suspend judgment, namely, on his skepticism! Why does he not doubt that he should be doubting values (for example, justice for all)? Second, some things ought not be doubted. Why should one doubt what seems obviously true, unless there is some good reason to do so? Further, ethics has to do with the way we live, and the skeptic cannot *live* skepticism. He cannot suspend all judgment on whether he should eat or drink, for example. And if he is married, he dare not suspend judgment on whether he should love his wife! In brief, there is no reason that one should allow skepticism to lead him to total relativism.

Relativism in the Middle Ages

Since the medieval period was dominated by a Christian point of view, one would not expect to see much ethical relativism. However, there are several Christian writers whose philosophy did contribute to ethical relativism.

Intentionalism. In the twelfth century, Peter Abelard argued that an act is right if it is done with good intention and wrong if done with bad intention.[5] Hence, some acts that seem bad are really not bad. We would not say, for example, that someone who accidentally killed another was morally culpable. Nor would we praise someone giv-

---

5. See Abelard, *Abelard's Ethics* III, trans. J. R. McCallum (Oxford: Blackwell, 1935), pp. 31-33.

ing money to the poor if he did so in order to be lauded of men. This being the case, it would seem that rightness or wrongness is determined solely by the intention of the person performing the action. Everything is relative to the person's intentions.

Perhaps the simplist way to state one objection to intentionalism is to point out the obvious truth that "the road to destruction is often paved with good intentions."[6] Even Hitler had "good" intentions for killing the Jews; he wanted to rid the world of the problem that plagued it (and in his view the problem was the Jews). Bad intentions will make an act wrong, but clearly good intentions will not necessarily make an act right. Intention is only one aspect of an ethical action. Another essential aspect is whether or not the intentions are in accord with what is intrinsically right (namely, a law or divine command).

Voluntarism. In the fourteenth century, William of Ockham argued that all moral principles are traceable to God's will (and that God could have decided otherwise about what is right and what is wrong).[7] If this is so, then whether or not one should love or hate is subject to change. Love could be right today and wrong tomorrow. Everything is relative to God's will, which can change. Many voluntarists take comfort in the fact that they believe God *will* not change His mind on essential ethical norms. This, however, will not suffice for several reasons.

The first difficulty with voluntarism is that it makes God arbitrary and not essentially good. Further, it exalts God's will above His nature and allows it to operate independently of His nature. This is questionable theology

---

6. Proverbs 14:12 reads, "There is a way which seems right to a man, but its end is the way of death" (RSV).

7. See William of Ockham, *Commentary on the Sentences* II, Prol., 1, BB.

at best. Further, voluntarism provides no security that
God will remain constant in His ethical concerns. Finally,
an act is not good simply because a sovereign power wills
it. It is good only if this power is a good power. Therefore,
tracing what is meant by right to God's will alone is not
sufficient; it must be traced to His good will, that is, to His
will acting in accordance with His good nature.

Nominalism. William of Ockham probably contributed
more to ethical relativisim than any other Christian
thinker in the Middle Ages. Ockham was a nominalist, or
one who denied the existence of universals.[8] Universals,
essences, or forms exist only conceptually, said Ockham, not actually. All reality is radically individual.
"Manness," for example, is only an abstract concept in
our minds. Individual men exist outside our minds, but
nowhere will one find "manness" existing anywhere
other than as a concept in a mind. It is not difficult to
see that if the same reasoning is applied to ethical con-
cepts such as goodness or justice, then they too would
exist only in a radically individual instance, but not in
any universal way. Hence, nominalism entails a radical
ethical relativism.

By way of criticism some have argued first that unless
there were common, universal forms of meaning, common
to all languages, then one could not translate meaning
from one language to another.[9] But universal communication does occur. Hence, there must be some "universals"
or universal basis for meaning. Second, others insist that
these universals must apply to all the particulars in their

8. See Ockham, *De principiis Theologiae* or the *Collectorium* of his
disciple, Gabriel Biel (d. 1495), whose work influenced Luther.
9. E. D. Hirsh says, "verbal meaning is determinate . . . it is an entity which is self-identical . . . it is an entity which always remains the
same from one moment to the next." *Validity in Interpretation* (New
Haven: Yale University Press, 1967), p. 46.

respective class, otherwise they would not be truly universal. Stated in ethical terms this would mean that all individually good acts must somehow partake of goodness, and that goodness is universal or common to all particular good acts. Finally, for the Christian there is a real basis for what is universally right—the nature of God. God is the absolute Ideal after which we should pattern our lives. Hence, it is doubly inappropriate for a Christian such as Ockham to claim there is no universal or essential good.

Relativism in the Modern World

Three relativistic ethical strains will be selected from the modern world to illustrate the growing trend toward relativism.

Utilitarianism. Jeremy Bentham (1748-1832) laid down the principle that one should act so as to produce the greatest good for the greatest number in the long run.[10] This is sometimes called the "utilitarian calculus." Our duty is to maximize good for the most people over the long run. Of course, the actions that may produce this result for most people at the moment will not necessarily be best for all persons nor for all times. In this sense utilitarianism is relativistic. Some utilitarians frankly admit that there may come a time when it would no longer be best to preserve life. That is, conditions may be such for some (or all) that it would be better not to live. In this case the greatest good would be to promote death.

The first problem with strict utilitarian relativism is that even it takes some things as universally true, for example, one should always act so as to maximize good. Second, utilitarian relativism implies that the end can justify

---

10. Jeremy Bentham, *Introduction to Principles of Morals and Legislation* (Oxford, 1789), l:1.

any means. What if a supposed good end, say, genetically purifying the race, demanded that we sterilize (or even kill) all "impure" genetic stock? Would this end justify the means of mercy-killing or forced sterilization? Surely not. Finally, results alone—even desired results—do not make something good. Sometimes what we desire is wrong. When the results are in, they must still be measured by some standard beyond them in order to know whether or not they are good.

Existentialism. Sören Kierkegaard (1813-1855) was the father of existentialism. Although he was a Christian thinker, he nonetheless opened the door to relativism by claiming that a man's highest duty (to God) sometimes transcends all ethical laws. Kierkegaard earnestly believed in the moral law which says, "Thou shalt not kill." However, he also held that when God said to Abraham, "Take your son Isaac and sacrifice him on the mountain," that Abraham was commanded to go beyond the ethical law in order to obey God.[11] There is no reason or justification for such an act, said Kierkegaard. One must simply perform this transcendent duty by "a leap of faith." Non-Christian existentialists since Kierkegaard are even more bold in proclaiming that each man has a right to "do his own thing." Jean-Paul Sartre (1905-1980) said, "It amounts to the same thing whether one gets drunk alone or is a leader of nations."[12]

Many criticisms are leveled at existential relativism. First, if everyone literally did his own "thing" it would lead to chaos, which would hinder everyone from doing anything. Second, even freedom needs a context or struc-

---

11. See Sören Kierkegaard, *Fear and Trembling* (New York: Double-day, 1954), esp. pp. 41, 57, 64f.
12. Jean-Paul Sartre, *Being and Nothingness* (New York: Washington Square Press, 1966), p. 767.

ture. Absolute freedom (of two or more persons) is impossible. If one man freely chooses to do to another man what that man freely does not want done to him there will be conflict. Law is intended to structure freedom in order to maximize one individual's rights without unfairly minimizing another's.[13] Third, unless there is some moral justification for an act, one is morally unjustified to perform it. No action escapes this ethical first principle of justice any more than a thought can escape the law of non-contradiction. Both thought and actions are governed by first principles. And he who breaks first principles will in the end be broken by them.

Evolutionism. After Darwin, men like Herbert Spencer (1820-1903) expanded evolution into a theory of cosmic development. Others, such as T. H. Huxley (1825-1895) and Julian Huxley (1887-1975), worked out an evolutionary ethic. It is ancient processism viewed evolutionarily. The central tenet of evolutionary ethics is that right is what aids the evolutionary development of mankind and wrong is what hinders it.

Julian Huxley laid down three principles of evolutionary ethics: (1) it is right to realize ever new possibilities in evolution; (2) it is right to respect human individuality and to encourage its fullest development; (3) it is right to construct a mechanism for further social evolution.[14] (He does not say what to do when 1 [or 3] conflicts with 2.) Such an ethic is obviously relativistic, since different behavior and attitudes will aid or hinder the evolutionary process at different times. Hence, right or wrong will be relative to a given stage of development.

---

13. See my *Christian Ethic of Love* (Grand Rapids: Zondervan, 1973), chapter 5.
14. Julian Huxley, *Collected Essays* (London, 1893-94), 9:46-116.

The objections to this ethic follow the lines of the objections to process and utilitarian views. First, who decides what the ultimate goal is? "Development" in which direction and in what way? Biologically, culturally, or politically? Further, how do we know desired "development" is actually good development? One can also develop or progress in evil. Finally, who decides what will "help or hinder" the progress, and what standards will be used? One must assume some standard outside the evolutionary process by which to judge; otherwise there is no way to know whether the project as a whole is really getting better or is simply different from a previous stage.[15] One can compare two things only by a third, unless one of the two is considered the absolute norm. But no one "stage" in the process is considered final. Hence, there must be a standard beyond it by which the stages are judged to be relatively good or bad.

Relativism in the Contemporary World

Several movements stand out in contemporary ethical relativism: emotivism, subjectivism, and situationism. In their extreme forms all of these are antinomianism.

Emotivism. A. J. Ayer (1910-1970) argued that all ethical statements are emotive.[16] "Thou shalt not . . ." really means "I feel it is wrong" or "I dislike it." Ethics is not prescriptive; it is simply emotive. Ethical pronouncements are merely ejaculations of our subjective feelings and not divine imperatives about moral duty. Clearly this is a radical relativism, since on these grounds everything would be relative to the vastly different feelings of different individuals.

---

15. C. S. Lewis makes this point in *Mere Christianity* (New York: Macmillan, 1964), chapter 5.

16. A. J. Ayer, *Language, Truth and Logic* (New York: Dover Publications, 1936), chapter 6.

The first difficulty with this view against moral pre-scriptions is that it is itself prescriptive. It legislates what must be meant by "ought" statements and insists they must be reduced to "I dislike" statements. However, in-stead of legislating what sentences must mean, we should listen to what they do mean. When one states, "Men ought not be racists," he really means that men ought not be such. Second, it has been observed that even emotivists do not actually believe that everything is relative; emotivists assume Hitler ought not have killed six million Jews. Even emotivists are not content simply to say "I feel Hitler was wrong, but someone else may feel that he was right." Finally, one who says he believes everything is relative to feelings will not *react* that way when he is the victim of an injustice. If an emotivist is cheated, robbed, or assaulted, his reaction will indicate that he really believes these activities are wrong.

Subjectivism. Jean-Paul Sartre's atheistic existen-tialism involved a form of radical subjectivism in ethics. He believed that there is no objective meaning or value to life. "Man is a useless passion," said Sartre. He also wrote, "There was nothing left in heaven, no right or wrong, nor anyone to give me orders. . . . I am doomed to have no other law but mine. . . . For I . . . am a man, and every man must find his own way."[17] Man is absolutely free and everything is relative to what the individual wills to do. We create our own meaning. There are no objective values to be discovered; all values are made subjectively by those who will them. Instead of a divine voluntarism (as in Ockham), Sartre held to a radically individual and human voluntarism.

By way of criticism it is important to observe, first, that

17. Jean-Paul Sartre, *No Exit and Three Other Plays,* "The Flies," (New York: Collier-Macmillan, 1966), pp. 121-23.

Sartre begins with a radical dichotomy of the subject and object. The basic reason that value cannot be objective is that a subject is not an object, and vice versa; indeed, never the twain shall meet. But this bifurcation is at the very least highly questionable. The Christian view of man declares that man is the subject who has objective value. Second, Sartre is inconsistent unless he recognizes that human freedom has objective value. For it is not only Sartre who is free, but all other persons are also free. But if all men are free—and not only Sartre himself—then this would mean that freedom is an objective reality in beings outside himself. For that is what is meant by "objective," namely, a reality independent of and outside of a subject (one's self). Finally, Sartre's position is actually antinomian and, as such, is subject to the criticisms of that position (see below).

Situationism. Joseph Fletcher's situational ethic exemplifies the relativistic position. Everything is relative to the situation, says Fletcher.[18] He says we should avoid "like the plague" absolutistic words such as "never," "always," "no," and "only." Even the Ten Commandments are only generally true, for Fletcher asserts there are exceptions to each and every command. In certain situations it is right to lie, steal, commit adultery, kill, and even blaspheme God. The only thing that is absolute, says Fletcher, is love. However, one cannot know what love means in advance of the situation. Love's decisions are made situationally, not prescriptively. Fletcher boldly proclaims that the end justifies the means. Thus if pregnancy were the only way to be released from prison, the end of being reunited with one's family would justify the means of committing adultery with the guard. Like-

---

18. See Joseph Fletcher, *Situation Ethics: The New Morality* (Philadelphia: Westminster Press, 1966), pp. 43-44.

wise, the end of saving your wife's life would justify the means of blaspheming God, and so on. In short, the situation determines what is right and what is wrong.

The first and most basic criticism of situationism is that it reduces to antinomianism; a single but contentless absolute is the same as *no* absolute at all. Commanding "love" in every situation without being able to define what "love" means is like commanding one to do X in every situation, when X is unknown. Further, Fletcher's view is plainly inconsistent when spelled out in straightforward English. "Avoid words such as 'never' and 'always' like the plague" really translates as, "One should never use the word 'never.' " Worse yet, it implies that "it is absolutely necessary to avoid all absolutes." But if one does not avoid universal statements in warning about universal statements, then his position is self-defeating. Finally, Fletcher does not heed his own warning to avoid universal words. He says love is the "only" norm for a Christian. Even in specific matters Fletcher uses universal language. On abortion he writes, *"No* unwanted baby should *ever* be born" (my emphasis).[19] Absolutes are, apparently, unavoidable.

Antinomianism

Few persons claim to be antinomian, but many actually are. The word *antinomian* comes from two Greek words, *anti* meaning "against" (or "instead of") and *nomos* meaning "law." So an antinomian is one who does not believe there are any ethical laws (and/or is actually against them). A. J. Ayer's and Jean-Paul Sartre's views were actually antinomian. Fletcher listed the early Christian Gnostics as antinomian, since they believed they had some special intuitive insight that went beyond all law.

Friedrich Nietzsche (1844-1900) is an example of an

---

19. Fletcher, *Situation Ethics*, p. 39.

antinomian, for he held that "God is dead" and all objective value died with Him. As in the title of one of his books, Nietzsche said we must go "beyond good and evil." He called himself "the first immoralist" who questioned even the most general of moral principles, such as, "Injure no man." Nietzsche most emphatically rejected the traditional "soft" Christian virtues. He would replace them with the "hard" virtues of the "superman."[20] But these virtues are not discovered; they are created by men with their "will-to-power."

There are several criticisms Christians give of complete relativity in ethics. First, one cannot absolutely deny all absolutes without thereby positing an absolute of his own. Either it is absolutely true that there are no absolutes or else there may be some absolutes. If the latter, then the door is open for one to proclaim an absolute. If the former, then there is an absolute, namely, one's denial that there are any absolutes.

Second, not everything can be in a state of constant and complete change. Change must be measured by what is not part of the change; otherwise one would not know any change had occurred. But what is not part of the changing world must be unchanging. Hence, change entails an absolute.

Third, everyone seems to have an "absolute" or "ultimate" in his system. As Paul Tillich (1886-1965) observed, everyone has an ultimate commitment, an unconditional center of his life. Without this center he would not be a person.[21] Sartre's absolute was "freedom." Neitzsche's was "will-to-power," or later, willing "eternal recurrence" of the same state of affairs. John Dewey

20. See Friedrich Nietzsche, *Beyond Good and Evil* (Chicago: Henry Regnery Co., 1966), sections 46, 262.

21. Paul Tillich, *Ultimate Concern* (London: SCM Press, 1965), p. 106.

(1859-1952) denied absolutes, but made "achievement" or "progress" his absolute. All one needs to do is discover what a man is unconditionally committed to, or passionately interested in—that is his ultimate or absolute. Finally, every person expects to be treated as a person. The proof that he really believes there are some unconditional values is that he expects his freedom and dignity to be respected. In his actions he may not always respect others, but in his reactions he proves that he always expects others to respect his freedom and dignity. Hence, human expectations are the key to what a man believes to be absolute.

Relativism and the Christian Options

Several observations should be made about relativism and Christian belief in ethical absolutes.

Total Relativism Is Unacceptable

There are many reasons that relativism is no option for a Christian. The two most basic reasons are as follows. First, as the above critique indicates, the arguments for total relativism are unsuccessful and often self-defeating. Second, the Bible declares that God is absolute and unchanging (Mal. 3:6; Heb. 13:8; 1:12), and that the moral law is a reflection of His unchanging character (cf. Matt. 5:48).

Total Absolutism Is Equally Unacceptable

Christianity is rightly absolutistic, since its ethic is based in the Absolute (God). However, total absolutism in every area is also unacceptable for Christians, for several reasons.

First, finite man does not have an absolute understanding of God's absolutes. Paul said, "Now we see through a glass, darkly" (I Cor. 13:12, KJV). That is, our understanding of God's perfect law is imperfect. God's Word is infallible (John 10:35), but our understanding of it is not. God in infinite by nature, but we have only a finite grasp of Him. Our understanding is adequate and sufficient, but it is not omniscient.

Second, not all biblical prescriptions are intended for all men at all times in all places (which is what is meant by an absolute). Some commands are not universal in extension, at least not in the need to obey them in all circumstances. The commands to obey parents or human government, for instance, are sometimes preempted by other, higher laws. Peter said, "We must obey God rather than men" (Acts 5:29). The three Hebrew children (Dan. 3) did not follow the command to obey human government (Rom. 13:1; I Peter 2:13).

Finally, not all ethical commands have equal weight. Jesus spoke of the "weightier matters of the law" (Matt. 23:23) and of the "greatest" and "least" commands (cf. Matt. 22:36). If this is so, a Christian must not legalistically follow the lesser commands when he is obligated to follow a greater one. Some obligations or commands are simply higher than others (cf. Matt. 22:36, 37).

Chapter 2

The Basis of Our Option

Revelation

For evangelicals the source of morality is God's revelation. When asked why we believe some things are right and others are wrong, we have but one answer: because God said so. How do we know what God has said? We know it because God has revealed it. God has revealed it both in nature (His general revelation) and in Scripture (His special revelation). God has written His law in our hearts (Rom. 2:12-15) and in His Word, the Bible (Ps. 19:7-14).

The Origin of Morality

Christian ethics originates with God and is based in His Word. It is an ethic of divine command.

The Ultimate Source of Morality: The Nature and Will of God

Unlike the changing social flux of most purely humanistic ethics, the Christian ethic is anchored ultimately and firmly in the unchanging nature of a God of

25

perfect love and justice. The Christian evades the false dichotomy of Bertrand Russell's charge that either ethics is based on God's arbitrary will or else God is Himself subject to something beyond Him.[1] The Christian recognizes a third alternative, that God's will is subject to His own unchanging nature. "I am the Lord, I change not" (Mal. 3:6, KJV). "The Glory of Israel will not lie or repent" (I Sam. 15:29). Indeed, Hebrews tells us that "it is impossible that God should prove false" (6:18).

To be sure, the Bible sometimes represents God as "repenting" or changing His mind (Gen. 6, Jonah 3), but this is because man has changed, and it *appears* from the human vantage point that God has changed. When one is riding into a wind he can say, "The wind is against me," and upon turning in the other direction proclaim, "The wind is with me." In fact the wind has not changed; the man has. Even so, in the unchanging "I Am" (Exod. 3:14) there "is no variation or shadow due to change" (James 1:17).

Not only is the Christian God immutable, but He is omnibenevolent. The Scriptures declare: "God *is* love" (I John 4:16). That is to say, love is of the very essence of God. It is for this reason that "God so loved the world that He gave His only Son, that whoever believes in Him should not perish but have eternal life" (John 3:16). In short, morality is based not in an arbitrary will of a supreme power (this is a humanistic distortion of the biblical God) but in the unchanging nature of a loving Father. The Christian God also has other attributes as well. He is just (Deut. 32:4), and we are assured that His love will be without "respect of persons" (Rom. 2:11). Indeed, it is for this reason that "God so loved the *world* . . ." and that He "is long-

---

1. Bertrand Russell, "Why I am not a Christian" in *The Basic Writing of Bertrand Russell*, ed. Robert E. Egner and Lester E. Dennon (New York: Simon and Schuster, 1961), p. 588.

suffering, not willing that any should perish, but that all should come to repentance" (II Peter 3:9, KJV).

The point here is not to give an exhaustive treatment of the attributes of God, but simply to note that Christian ethics is based in the will of God who acts in accord with His unchanging character, loving justice, and just love. God is neither arbitrary in His will nor subjected, like Plato's Demiurge, to something outside Himself which is more ultimate than He. God's will is subjected only to what is inside Himself, that is, to the unchanging loving and holy character of His own essence.

The Revelation of God's Will

The Christian believes that God has revealed Himself in two spheres available to men: in His world (including mankind) and in His Word (the Scriptures). The former is sometimes called "natural revelation" and the latter, "supernatural revelation." Sometimes these two revelations of God are called, respectively, "general" (since it is available to all men) and "special" (since it is particular, focused, and specific information available to those who have access to a Bible or its truths).

God's revelation in nature and the human heart. Since in the providence of God He knew that not all men would have access to the truths of Scripture at all times, He inscribed a law upon their hearts. The apostle Paul wrote, "When Gentiles who have not the law do by nature what the law requires, they are a law to themselves, even though they do not have the [written] law. They show that what the law requires is written on their hearts, while their conscience also bears witness . . ." (Rom. 2:14, 15). Some Christian thinkers have described this as "innate" or as "a natural inclination."[2] It is often called the

---

2. Thomas Aquinas, *Summa Theologica* I. 103. 8.

"natural law." Even some humanists admit to the universality of ethical principles. A few even boldly replace the law of the eternal God with what they call "uncreated nature." Others are more cautious.

The moral creeds of mankind's great civilizations have given testimony to the general revelation of God by manifesting striking resemblance in their basic moral principles. C. S. Lewis has assembled many of these in an excellent appendix to his book, The Abolition of Man.[3] Further evidence of the universal availability of God's "natural revelation" comes to light when one asks the following questions. What person does not expect to be treated as a person? Whoever has actually held that it was right to take what belonged to anyone at any time? Whoever actually believed that rape or cruelty to children was morally right? To be sure, mankind has not always lived up to its moral ideas—this is an indication of our depravity and need for Christ's redemption—but one's true moral principles cannot always be discovered from what one does. A man does sometimes break his own moral principles. A Christian believes in the Golden Rule (Matt. 7:12), but what Christian (or non-Christian) perfectly practices it? Indeed, it is not what men do, but what they believe (or say) ought to be done that is a closer clue to the natural law within them. Hence, it is in the great moral creeds of mankind and perhaps even more so in their deep-seated beliefs that we may discover God's general revelation.

Of course, even in moral creeds we may expect some divergence. Man's finitude, as well as his sinfulness, can account for much diversity of interpretation. After all, scientists have been studying for thousands of years the

---

3. C. S. Lewis, The Abolition of Man (New York: Macmillan Co., 1962), pp. 95-121.

same objective world and often have come to very different interpretations of it. It should not be surprising, then, that the objective and universal moral world (i.e., God's natural revelation) should be viewed somewhat differently by different men at different times. There is, nonetheless, a surprising amount of unanimity of understanding of "natural revelation" indicated by the great moral creeds of mankind.

There is an even deeper indication of the universality of the moral law of God than human creeds; it is the expectations of human hearts. It is not in what people do or even in what they say ought to be done; rather, it is in what they expect others to do to them. If one wants to know whether it is right to take another's property (or even his mate) at any time, do not ask him what he wishes to do or what he says one has the right to do. Just watch carefully how he reacts when someone attempts to seize what he loves dearly. In this sense the moral law can be discovered more by one's reactions than by his actions. Surely it is fallacious to argue, as many humanists do, that what people do is what they ought to do. One can no more legitimately move from "do" to "ought" than he can from "is" to "ought," as Hume and others have pointed out.

The problem that humanists must face is this: once one rejects the belief in a personal God who prescribes a moral "ought" and is left only with the evolving social web of what people actually do as the result of the interplay of their desires, how can one ever get from this social "do" to a moral "ought?"

Ironically, non-Christian humanists often act as though their ethical obligations were personal (i.e., directed to a Person), but they say that they are not. Julian Huxley, for example, refused to be comforted upon the death of his son by the doctrine of immortality because he felt he could not "play fast and loose with truth." But as one Christian writer has aptly observed,

> We do not feel shame or pollution when we harm *things* or even when we transgress impersonal *laws*, but we do feel these when we violate the rights of *persons*. Why should men like Clifford and Huxley be so finicky about the "truth" if there is nothing in the world but matter and our feeble lives? Their carefulness becomes fully rational, however, *if there is One to whom their dishonesty becomes disloyalty*. The practice of the honest atheist frequently denies the conscious import of his words, because he is acting in a way which makes no sense *unless his conscious conclusions are untrue*.[4]

But once a humanist denies God, logically he is left without anything he "ought" to do. On the other hand, according to the Scriptures, God's voice speaks to the hearts of all men, even those who have not the written law of God. Paul wrote, "All who have sinned without the [written] law will also perish without the law, and all who have sinned under the [written] law will be judged by the law" (Rom. 2:12).

Before we leave God's revelation in nature, it is worth noting that it is this common revelation with non-Christian humanists that makes moral cooperation with non-Christians possible. If there were nothing but a special revelation (such as that in Scripture), as regrettably some theologians have claimed (Karl Barth, for example), then there would be no meeting place. All one could do is shout his view from the pinnacle of his own revelational presupposition at his benighted nonrevelational humanistic counterpart. And all the humanist could do is reciprocate from his totally diverse and isolated standpoint. Thanks to God's general revelation this is not necessary. Even non-Christian humanists who explicitly reject God's revelation in Scripture operate nonetheless in the sphere

---

4. David Elton Trueblood, *Philosophy of Religion* (New York: Harper, 1957), p. 108, 115 (my emphasis).

of God's natural revelation. Hence, both common light and common morals are available for cooperative efforts with nonbelievers.

Another important aspect of God's general revelation is that it enables a Christian to maintain an ethical standard and to explain how non-Christians can sense the same duty without accepting the Bible. Indeed, since the moral law is available in the human milieu without any explicit theistic connections, one can even believe in the moral law without being a theist. This being the case, no humanist can justifiably charge that adopting the Christian point of view entails rejecting the possibility of any ethical standard for non-Christians. The moral law is available to the non-Christian whether or not he admits there is a moral law Giver, in the same way that the creation is available to all men whether or not they explicitly admit there is a Creator.

God's revelation in Scripture. In addition to general revelation, the Christian believes there is a special revelation in Scripture. The Bible claims to be the divinely inscripturated truth of God (II Tim. 3:16, 17). It is a special revelation of the same moral character of God revealed in nature and the hearts of men.

This immediately raises the question, Why does God have two revelations? Was the first one insufficient? If so, why? If not, then is the second revelation redundant? There are two basic reasons for God to add His supernatural revelation to the natural one. First, the supernatural revelation is necessary to overcome the effects of sin on the minds of fallen men, and second, it provides more information about God than does natural revelation. Since these two are related we will treat them together. "Sin came into the world through one man and death through sin, and so death spread to all men because all men sinned" (Rom. 5:12). Through sin the minds of men are darkened (Eph. 4:18); therefore, special light is needed to illuminate man's mind to the truth revealed in the natural world but which his sin has obscured. Were it not for sin there would have been no need for either supernatural revelation or redemption through Christ.

Further, God's special revelation is more clear and explicit than the first. Indeed, special revelation is not only higher in kind but it is greater in extent. One can know more truths via special revelation than through general revelation. For example, most evangelical Christians believe that the so-called "mysteries" of the faith, such as the Trinity and the incarnation of Christ, are not known by natural revelation alone.

Likewise, most evangelicals hold that natural revelation is sufficient only to reveal the moral standard for man, but that it is not sufficient for man's salvation (cf. Rom. 1:19, 20 and 2:12). It is generally agreed, however, that if one follows the light he has, then God will give him the added (supernatural) light he needs to be saved. As Peter put it, "In every nation anyone who fears him [God] and does what is right is acceptable to him" (Acts 10:35). This was said when God sent Peter with the gospel to the Gentile, Cornelius, who was seeking God. In this regard the Book of Hebrews informs us that "whoever would draw near to God must believe that he exists and that he rewards those who seek him" (11:6). Of course, those who do not seek God's light find themselves in darkness: "Men loved darkness rather than light, because their deeds were evil" (John 3:19). But anyone anywhere who chooses to know and to do the will of God, to him will God reveal Himself—whether through a preacher of the gospel (Rom. 10:14), or through a dream or vision (Dan. 2), or by an angel (Rev. 14), or through the Scriptures themselves (Heb. 4:12).

The point of special revelation in Scriptures is simply this: God has revealed Himself to all men through natural creation, "for what can be known about God is plain to them, because God has shown it to them" (Rom. 1:19). The problem is man's sin, and for this reason "the wrath of God is revealed from heaven against all ungodliness of men who by their wickedness suppress the truth (v. 18). In view of man's sin, which has darkened his mind and obscured the light of God's natural revelation which would shine through the windows of his soul, God has given a special revelation to aid in overcoming these noetic effects of sin. In this regard, the natural revelation to a fallen man is like the occasional lightning that illuminates the landscape under the storm of sin—it momentarily but clearly reveals what is there. However, these flashes of light are not as great as the sustained noonday sun of special revelation.

Special revelation gives more detailed and explicit light from God for direction in a believer's life. But for those who are by their own choice spiritually nocturnal, God provides darkness in accord with that choice. As the apostle Paul wrote, "If our gospel is veiled, it is veiled only to those who are perishing. In their case the god of this world has blinded the minds of unbelievers, to keep them from seeing the light of the gospel of the glory of Christ . . ." (II Cor. 4:3, 4). But believers who want the special revelation of God proclaim, "Thy word is a lamp to my feet and a light to my path" (Ps. 119:105).

In short, the Scriptures provide more specific information and instruction for those who freely choose to know more about the light. For any who prefer to stay bound in the cave of their own decisions, there is ever the darkened world of flickering natural light. But such shadows fade as one moves away from the cave toward more light through the Scriptures.

There are numerous advantages of an inscripturated revelation. It is more clear, more precise, more easily promulgated without distortion, and less subject to misunderstanding and misrepresentation than is intuitively known revelation. In these and other ways the Scriptures are more definitive and specific in the declaration of God's moral will for the lives of men. That is, the Bible provides an objectively knowable referent point for discovering the will of the immutably loving and just God. To be sure, Scripture—like any other objective declaration—can be misunderstood, misapplied, and even twisted. But abuse does not bar use. Some objectively declared law is better than none, even if men do distort it. Likewise, it is better that God has objectively declared Himself in Scripture than that He has not (more on this in chapter four).

The Nature of Morality

The evangelical has a decided advantage over the non-Christian humanist on the question of the nature of morality. This is obvious for several reasons.

Morality Is Objective, Not Subjective

The strict humanist struggles to make men's subjective choices and desires sound objective. At best, however, they can only describe what men desire, not what men ought to do. Moral laws are only "binding" when non-Christian humanists accept them as binding. Should they come to reject moral principles—whether those principles prohibit rape, cruelty, or murder—then they are no longer binding. The humanist can merely hold, "Thus saith men, and it may change"; he cannot say, "Thus saith the Lord, who cannot change."

Some humanists frankly assert that all ethics are simply emotive.[5] They reduce "thou shalt" to "I feel."

---

5. See A. J. Ayer, *Language, Truth and Logic* (New York: Dover Publications, 1936), chapter six.

Hence, "thou shalt not commit murder" means "I don't like murder." It seems obvious enough that an ejaculation of one's feelings is less than adequate as a basis of morality. Racism, cruelty, and hatred are not wrong simply because some (or even all) men *feel* this way at a given stage in their social evolution. They are wrong because by their very nature these things ought not be done. While not all humanists would agree with Ayer's complete emotivism, it is difficult for them to avoid it without holding to an objective and absolute standard outside of human desires. And for those few humanists who claim there is an absolute moral law outside man, it is difficult to avoid the conclusion that there is an absolute moral law Giver outside of man.

Morality Has an Absolute Basis

The Christian has no problem with this dilemma, for absoluteness is a distinctive characteristic of evangelical ethics. This absolute basis for morality is found in an infinitely perfect God who wills men to be good in accordance with the unchanging perfection of His own nature. "You, therefore, must be perfect, as your heavenly Father is perfect" (Matt. 5:48). One of the incongruities of the contemporary taste for relativism is that relativists seem absolutely certain that relativism is true. Humanism has often championed relativism but has seldom appreciated the absolute(s) it harbors in its own bosom; namely the belief in the absolute character of its own humanistic presuppositions. Ironically, many non-Christian forms of humanism conceal absolutes in their own cellars that were borrowed from the Judeo-Christian Scriptures. In essence, much (if not all) of the value of humanism is derived from the Christian character of their premises or presuppositions. In this moral sense, Western humanisms are often kind of nontheistic Christian cults. It is strange how Bertrand Russell could write in *Why I Am Not a Christian* an attack on the very character of Christ and yet admit later, "What the world needs is Christian love or compassion."[6] The Christian will simply ask, How can we have Christian love without *Christ?* The Christian asserts that God is absolute, Christ is God in human flesh, and we have had an expression of God's absolute character propositionalized in His Word (the Bible). But can the humanist borrow the ethic of Christ without the Christ of the ethic? It would seem that the dilemma of humanism is this: either admit relativism, or acknowledge absolutism as is embodied in the Christian ethic. In the Christian ethic there is no need to avoid absolutes and there certainly is a place to ground them, namely, in an unchanging God.

Morality Is Normative, Not Utilitarian

There is a marked difference between Christianity and non-Christian humanism at this point. Many humanists are confessedly utilitarian, deciding what one ought to do on the basis of what they believe will bring the greatest happiness to the greatest number of people in the long run. The Christian can respond to this by noting that only God could be a successful utilitarian, since only He knows the long run. In any event, Christians believe that it is our responsibility to keep the rules and God's responsibility to take care of the results. Surely an all-good and all-knowing God is the only one in a position to know which rules will bring the best results. The best that men can do is experiment by trial and error, and thus build useful ethical rules of thumb. But they can never be certain future experience will not disconfirm these rules, nor that these are indeed the best rules to bring about the best

---

6. Bertrand Russell, *Human Society in Ethics and Politics* (New York: Mentor, 1962), p. iii.

results over the long haul. Only a sure word from God can guarantee this.

Morality Is Discovered, Not Created by Men

One marked distinctive of the Christian ethic is the tenet that man does not create basic ethical values; he simply discovers them. It is God who determines ethical values. By this we do not mean to imply that men are not free to accept or reject the values God has determined. Men are indeed free to reject God's law; herein is their depravity. The God-given values nonetheless exist, and the non-Christian finds it difficult—if not impossible—to live without them.

Some non-Christians have wrongly insisted that if we discover values in a normal psychological and sociological way (which we apparently do), then the values cannot be absolute: they are based in a relative social process. This objection, however, confuses the social *context* of values with their actual *basis*. Simply because we learn mathematics, for example, through a relative social process does not mean that all mathematical truths are based on what is socially relative.

The Superiority of the Christian View of Right

From the foregoing discussion, we see a number of values of the Christian ethic that characterize it as superior to any other ethic.

A Superior Source: God

The Christian claims God is an infinitely loving, personal Being whose perfections are absolute. Even the most optimistic non-Christian humanism can only offer an admittedly inferior human species which is hopefully and emergently being perfected by trial and error. If the Christian claim is correct, then the ultimate source of its morality (in the character of God) is infinitely superior to any mere humanistic ethic. It would seem that even the non-Christian would have to admit this.

There is a logical consequence here that humanists have not fully faced. If an infinite value is of greater value than a finite value, then the only way a humanist can argue that his ethic—based in man—is superior, is to demonstrate that the Christian God does not exist. But all attempts to disprove God have been notoriously unsuccessful. Indeed, many such attempts boomerang, for they are inconsistent.[7]

A Superior Personal Manifestation: Christ

The Bible teaches that Christ is God incarnate in human flesh (John 1:1; Heb. 1:8; Col. 1:16, 17; and so forth). The New Testament proclaims Him to be the Jehovah of the Old Testament on numerous occasions (cf. Rev. 11:17 with Isa. 41:4, and Phil. 2:10 with Isa. 45:23). Jesus Himself claimed to be the "I Am" of Exodus 3:14 (John 8:58) and to be the eternal partner of God's glory (John 17:5), which Isaiah 42:8 says Jehovah will never give to another. Jesus claimed to be able to forgive sins and raise the dead, which elicited outcries of blasphemy from the monotheistic Jews to whom He spoke (Mark 2:7 and John 5:25f., cf. 8:59). Jesus accepted worship on numerous occasions (cf. Matt. 28:17 and John 9:38). Often when he made these claims the Jews picked up stones to kill Him, saying, "We stone you for no good work but for blasphemy: because you, being a man, make yourself God" (John 10:33).

In view of the unique, miraculous fulfillment of dozens of prophecies uttered hundreds of years before His birth, many of which Jesus could not possibly have manipulated,

---

7. See Norman L. Geisler and Paul D. Feinberg, *Introduction to Philosophy* (Grand Rapids: Baker Book House, 1980), chapter 19.

such as the time and place of His birth (Dan. 9 and Mic. 5); and in view of His sinless and miraculous life, and His supernatural resurrection from the grave (which is historically verifiable), the most reasonable conclusion is to accept Christ's claim about Himself to be God. Numerous skeptics have examined these claims in the light of historical and legal evidence and have been converted to Christianity.[8] The claims are still open for examination today.

In the light of Christ's deity and His incarnation, the Christian possesses an ethical manifestation superior to any mere humanism. He who was God Himself was one of us and lived among us, showing us how to live with ourselves. Humanism as such has never produced even a perfect man, let alone the God-man. Christianity presents the second Person of the Godhead who became man and dwelt among us (John 1:14). Jesus is the One "who in every respect has been tempted as we are, yet without sinning" (Heb. 4:15). Jesus was truly human in every sense of the word. He ate and slept; He experienced hunger, fatigue, and anger; He knew loneliness and suffering. And it is because of all this that we have a personal and human referent—a perfect one—for our morality. Christ is our complete moral example. In view of Him, morality is not a mere legalistic assent to a written code; it is a dynamic relation to a living person. The essence of morality is not the love of abstract laws; it is the love of a concrete person (Jesus Christ), and through Him and by Him the love of all persons (Matt. 22:36, 37). The Christian ethic, then, is eminently human and personal in its manifestation.

A Superior Ethical Declaration: The Bible

God is love. Christ is God's love manifest in personal

---

8. See Frank Morrison, *Who Moved the Stone?* (Downers Grove, Ill.: InterVarsity, 1958).

form. The Law or written Word of God is love manifest in propositional form. The Bible as God's "love letter" is a way of expressing love. Love can be expressed in more than actions; it can be expressed, as any lover or poet knows, in words. Moral laws, then, are God's way of putting love into words. Indeed, Jesus said that all of the moral laws of the Old Testament are merely expressions of two loves, one for God and one for man (Matt. 22:36, 37).

Law, then, for the Christian, is a propositional statement of personal concern that calls for personal loving response. But this love cannot be forced down people's throats; love can be commanded, but it cannot be demanded. That is, moral laws can tell us what is best for us and exhort us to do it (and surely an infinitely wise and loving God knows this better than we do), but moral laws cannot force us to conform. Love always leaves space to say, "No, thank you." So while moral laws have a positive force they cannot in this sense have a positive enforcement. Laws indicate the direction that is best for the true happiness of the individual, but they do not dictate.

A Superior Motivation: The Love of Christ

Non-Christian humanists are often self-conscious about humanism's lack of motivation to perform what it holds to be moral rules or goals. Indeed, it might be said that they are often correct about the general moral laws (or at least the goal) but cannot generate the motivation from within their humanism to keep those laws.

This is not surprising to the Christian who remembers the words of Paul, "For God has done what the law, weakened by the flesh, could not do: sending His own Son in the likeness of sinful flesh and for sin, he condemned sin in the flesh, in order that the just requirement of the law might be fulfilled in us, who walk not according to the flesh but according to the Spirit" (Rom. 8:3, 4). The moral law was never intended to make man moral, any more than yardsticks are made to make people grow taller or plumblines are made to straighten buildings. The law was simply given to show us God's standard. By the same token, when we fall short of the law we do not use the standard itself as a corrective. A mirror will show one how dirty his face is, but it is not intended to be used as a washcloth to remove the dirt.

The law reveals man's condemnation before a Holy God in the light of His moral standards, but the law cannot save. In this sense, the law brings condemnation but not salvation. Only Christ can save. But here is precisely the point of superiority in the Christian system. Where does one get the motivation to love others in accordance with God's love? What motivated the great social movements that started hospitals, launched the Red Cross, established rescue missions, improved working conditions, and sent thousands to the underdeveloped nations with strategic help? In numerous social efforts it was Christians motivated by the love of Christ who provided the needed energy to accomplish these tasks. It was men and women who said in essence, "The love of Christ controls us, because we are convinced that one has died for all; therefore. . . . those who live might live no longer for themselves but for him who for their sake died and was raised" (II Cor. 5:14, 15).

Chapter 3

Option One

Unqualified Absolutism

Perhaps the most influential and widely held view among Christians is that of unqualified absolutism. The position received its classic presentation in Augustine and has been defended by notable philosophers such as Immanuel Kant and by theologians such as John Murray and Charles Hodge.

An Exposition of Unqualified Absolutism

The basic premise of unqualified absolutism is that all moral conflicts are only *apparent;* they are not real. Sin is always avoidable. There are moral absolutes that admit of no exceptions and these never actually come into conflict with one another. On the classic question as to whether or not one should ever lie to save a life, the unqualified absolutist answers with an emphatic, no! The importance of this issue to Augustine can be measured by the fact that he dedicated two works to it, *Against Lying* and *On Lying,* plus numerous other references throughout his writings.

Augustine's Unqualified Absolutism

The medieval bishop Augustine has sometimes been misunderstood to be a situationist because of his statement that one should "love God and do as he will." While it is true that Augustine cast his whole ethical system in terms of love, it is not true that he held to only one love command. Augustine believed that "charity [love] consummates the virtues, it does not consume them." Rather, "charity implies the other virtues and takes them for granted."[1]

Augustine's arguments against lying. There are many arguments offered by Augustine against ever breaking the moral absolute of truth-telling. We will first summarize them and then give an evaluation of them.

Augustine is quick to point out that not all falsifications are lies. Only those falsifications with intention to deceive qualify as lies. "A person is to be judged as lying or not lying according to the intention of his mind, not truth or falsity of the matter itself."[2] Thus something said in jest or even something false, spoken by one who intends the hearer to understand something true by it, is not a lie. For example, if a man wants to reach a certain city, and asks directions of a friend he knows is a perpetual liar, the liar should give him directions that take him along the bandit-infested route. That way the friend will take the opposite route and avoid the robbers and possible death. This is not a lie.

One should never lie even to save a life, to avoid a sin, or even to save a soul. Augustine makes this crystal clear in many arguments.

---

1. Quoted in E. Gilson, *History of Christian Philosophy* (Westminster, Md., Christian Classics, reprint), p. 141.
2. Augustine, *On Lying* 3. 3.

(1) One should never sin to avoid sin. Lying to ward off rape or even to save a life is strictly forbidden by Augustine's unqualified absolutism, for one's choice is really between "the permission of the sin of another, or the commission of one's own sin."[3] Of a certain heretical group, the Priscillianists, who were lying to keep themselves from being discovered, Augustine insisted that Christians ought to condemn the impiety (lying) as well as the heresy. Further, Christians ought not lie to expose liars. In short, committing one sin to avoid another sin is still a sin.

(2) One should not sin in order to attain a greater good. Some had suggested that lying would be permissible as a means of getting another to heaven. But Augustine insisted that no eternal good could be accomplished by a temporal evil. He wrote, "Let it not be supposed that for any reason whatsoever a lie ought to be told in such matters, since not even to bring anyone more readily to a knowledge of the truth may falsehood be introduced into that teaching."[4]

(3) Lying destroys all certainty. Lying breaks down regard for the truth and "when regard for the truth has been broken down or even slightly weakened, all things will remain doubtful, unless these are believed to be true, they cannot be considered as certain."[5] In brief, without truth-telling there is no integrity and without integrity there can be no certainty. For once falsity is ever admitted into communication, then one can never again be certain the speaker is telling the truth.

(4) Lying is a web that entangles more and more. Lying necessitates more lying to explain and cover up for itself. Eventually, argued Augustine, this will lead to perjury or

---

3. Ibid., 20. 41.
4. Ibid., 10. 19.
5. Ibid.

even blasphemy. For if one becomes a habitual liar, then he might lie even to God.

(5) Lying would weaken the Christian faith. For if we be untruthful in one area then how can people believe us when we teach them Christian doctrine? When teaching the faith to them they will say, "Whence then do I know whether thou art not doing it even now . . .?"[6]

(6) Sins of the soul are worse than sins of the body. Augustine borrowed a platonic premise as a basis for his argument that one should never lie even to avoid rape. One should endeavor to preserve chastity in both soul and body, "but when both cannot be so protected, who does not realize which one should be guarded at the expense of the other . . .?" He continues, saying that everyone "realizes full well which should be preferred to the other; the soul to the body, or the body to the soul. . . ."[7]

(7) Lying condemns men to hell. Augustine cites numerous passages from the Bible (and Apocrypha) to support his unqualified absolutism. Psalm 5:5, 6 is rendered, "Thou dost hate, O Lord, all who work iniquity; thou shalt destroy all who speak a lie." Wisdom 1:11 is also quoted by Augustine, "The mouth that belieth, killeth the soul." Thus Augustine concludes that "since eternal life is lost by lying, a lie may never be told for the preservation of the temporal life of another."[8]

(8) Truth-telling is good. Augustine admitted that some acts were not good or bad in themselves. For example, giving to the poor is good at some times and bad at other times, depending on the motive for giving. "But, when the works themselves are already sin, such as theft, impurity, blasphemy, and the like, who would say that they should be done for good reasons so as either not to be sins or

---

6. Augustine, *Against Lying*, 7.
7. Augustine, *On Lying*, 20. 41.
8. Ibid., 6. 9.

else, still more absurd, to be just sins?"[9] Some moral acts are intrinsically good and, hence, their violation can never be for a good purpose.

In his *Retractions* Augustine confessed that some of his arguments were "obscure," but he never revised or corrected them. He went to his reward firmly believing in an unqualified moral absolutism.

Augustine's treatment of allegedly justified lies in Scripture. On the face of it, the Bible seems to record many cases of justified lying. Augustine was aware of these passages and attempted to explain them in terms of his unqualified absolutism.

(1) Rahab and the Hebrew midwives. The Hebrew midwives lied to the king, and yet God apparently blessed them for it (Exod. 1). Rahab's lie saved the Jewish spies, and she is commended for her faith in the Book of Hebrews "Hall of Fame" (chap. 11). Augustine's answer was that God blessed these women for their mercy but did not condone their impiety. God did not praise them "because they lied but because they were merciful to the men of God. And so, it was not their deception that was rewarded, but their benevolence; the benignity of their intention, not the iniquity of their invention."[10]

(2) Lot's dilemma. Lot faced a moral conflict when the Sodomites demanded his guests for immoral purposes. To some, Lot's action of giving his daughters to appease the Sodomites seemed like an avoidance of a greater sin (homosexuality) by allowing a lesser one (rape)—a position which Augustine rejected. The Bishop replied to this dilemma by reminding them of two things. First, one must never commit "a great crime of your own in your horror for someone else's greater crime."[11] Second, and more

---

9. Augustine, *Against Lying*, 7. 18.
10. Ibid., 15. 32.
11. Ibid., 9. 22.

directly to the point of the dilemma, Augustine insisted that Lot did not himself sin but allowed the Sodomites to sin by raping his daughters.

(3) David's oath to kill Nabal. The Bible seems to say that an oath before God is inviolable (see Eccles. 5:1-6), and yet the Bible (and common sense) would seem to suggest that one should not keep a foolish or sinful oath. Augustine's answer is that "it is clear that we should not make part of our manners everything that we read has been done by righteous or just men."[12] In short, the Bible records but does not approve of David's action of making such a sinful oath.

(4) Abraham and Jacob's alleged lies. The Scriptures say that Abraham claimed Sarah to be his "sister" (she was his half-sister) in order to protect himself from being killed if the king discovered she was his wife (Gen. 20). Augustine insisted that Abraham was not lying since "he only concealed something of the truth but did not say anything that was false. . . ."[13] As to Jacob's alleged deception of his father Isaac in order to obtain God's blessing, Augustine argues that "what Jacob did at his mother's bidding, in seeming to deceive his father, is not a lie but a mystery."[14]

(5) Jesus' alleged deceptions. The Gospel account tells us that Jesus asked, "Who touched me?" as though he didn't know; later he indicated to the two disciples on the Emmaus road that he would go farther when he had no intention of doing so (Luke 24:28). Augustine's answer here is that this was not really deception but instruction. "He pretended not to know [who touched his garment] in order that He might signify something else by that apparent ignorance of His. Since this significance was true,

---

12. Ibid.
13. Ibid., 10. 23.
14. Ibid., 10. 24.

it surely was not a lie."[15] This answer seems to imply that as long as one conveys what is true in the light of his intentions, even if some deception is (necessarily) involved in so doing, then he has not lied. John Murray will develop this point later.

Kant's Unqualified Absolutism

Immanuel Kant was one of the most influential thinkers of modern times. He was agnostic about knowing reality-in-itself, but he was a devout believer in God and was a moral absolutist.

Kant's categorical imperative. Kant eschewed any hypothetical ethics such as "*if* one does this, then this or that will result." He favored a categorical "one *ought* to do thus and thus." Duties are duties regardless of the consequences. This central moral obligation is called the *categorical imperative.* Kant stated this principle several ways. First, we should always treat others as an end and never as a means to an end. And second, one should act so that he could will his action a rule for all men.

Examples of the categorical imperative. Kant felt that both lying and murder were universally wrong. That is, it could never be one's duty either to lie or to kill. His justification for this position is as follows. If one were to will lying as a universal rule, then there would be no more truth to lie about. Hence, it would be self-destructive to lie. But whatever we cannot will as a universal rule we should never do, for this is what the categorical imperative demands. Likewise, one should never kill, for if he does so then he must will that all can kill. But if all kill, then there will be no one left to kill. Therefore, murder should never be permitted in even one instance.

---

15. Ibid., 13. 27-28.

Should one ever lie to avoid murder? The fact that one should neither lie nor murder leads to the dilemma that Kant addressed in his tractate, "On the Supposed Right to Lie from Benevolent Motives." His response to that supposition, like Augustine's response, was a categorical no. He wrote, "Whoever then tells a lie, however good his intentions may be, must answer for the consequences of it . . . however unforeseen they may have been." For "to be truthful (honest) in all declarations is therefore a sacred unconditional command of reason, and not to be limited by any expediency."[16]

Kant's reasons. There are at least three reasons stated or implied by Kant for his unqualified absolutism.

First, moral duties by their very nature admit no exceptions. Any exception would indicate that it was not truly a rule. Moral laws, like Newton's law of gravitation, Kant believed, had no exceptions.

Second, moral duties are intrinsic, not extrinsic, and whatever is intrinsically good cannot be evil. It is as absurd to call an intrinsically good act evil as it is to call light darkness. Only what is neither good nor bad in itself (but its goodness or evil depends on something else) can be called evil at one time and good at another. But intrinsically good actions are not like this; they are always good in and of themselves. Since telling the truth is an intrinsic good and a lie is an intrinsic evil, there can never be a good lie.

The third argument implied by Kant for the inviolable nature of a moral duty is that it is self-destructive to hold otherwise. Although this argument may seem to be kind of a pragmatic one—and, hence, contrary to Kant's own belief that duties are not determined by consequences—it

---

16. *Kant's Critique of Practical Reason,* ed. Francis Abbot (London: Longmans, Green and Co., Ltd., 1909), p. 268.

actually is not. In fact, the argument is a kind of transcendental argument which goes like this: it is absolutely necessary to posit moral duties as categorical and universal in order to live. A pragmatic argument says only that certain consequences are more desirable than others, and these we call good. Kant insists that the moral law is based on what is rationally necessary to posit for life, not what is simply socially or personally desirable.

John Murray's Unqualified Absolutism

One of the best examples of unqualified absolutism in the evangelical tradition is that of John Murray of Westminster Seminary. In his book, *Principles of Conduct*, Murray elaborates how he would maintain "the sanctity of truth" even in situations which would seem to call for a justifiable lie.

God's law is absolute. Like Augustine, John Murray believes that God's law is absolutely binding. The will of God is a sovereign reflection of God's character. Since God is truth and cannot ever lie, then neither should we. The moral standard in Scripture is: "Be ye therefore perfect, even as your Father which is in heaven is perfect" (Matt. 5:48, KJV).

Lying is always wrong. Because the command to tell the truth flows from the absolute law of God, we can make no exceptions to it. Murray wrote, "The necessity of truthfulness in us rests upon God's truthfulness. As we are to be holy because God is holy, so we are to be truthful because God is truthful."[17]

Explanation of alleged biblical lies. Murray offers an explanation for some of the difficult biblical passages

---

17. John Murray, *Principles of Conduct* (Grand Rapids: Eerdmans, 1957), p. 127.

along the same lines as Augustine. With regard to Rahab he says, "Although our purpose be to assist our brethren, to consult for their safety and to relieve them, it never can be lawful to lie, because that cannot be right which is contrary to the nature of God."[18] After reviewing several biblical examples of lying Murray concludes, "We see, therefore, that neither Scripture itself nor the theological inferences derived from Scripture provide us with any warrant for the vindication of Rahab's untruth and this instance, consequently, does not support the position that under certain circumstances we may justifiably utter an untruth."[19]

Charles Hodge: "Modified" Unqualified Absolutism

Charles Hodge offered a significant modification to unqualified absolutism which enables the position to admit there are some genuine moral conflicts but deny there are any absolute ones.

Some absolutists in this tradition are willing to make a distinction between commands based on God's *nature* (which admit no exceptions or change) and those based on God's *will* (which can have exceptions and change). If valid, this distinction would permit some real conflicts in commands and yet insist that only one of the two commands in conflict (the one based on God's nature) is actually absolute. To be consistent, an unqualified absolutist holding this view would also have to maintain that no two moral principles based on God's nature could ever really conflict. It is not clear what Hodge would say on this point.

One Final Point: The Providence of God

Ethical absolutists of the variety discussed here often imply and sometimes state another ingredient of their

---

18. Ibid., p. 139.
19. Ibid.

view, namely, the providence of God. They admit that persons are sometimes faced with moral dilemmas in which, unless God acts to deliver them, whatever they do would be evil. However, there is a way "out," namely, to trust the miraculous intervention of God. Several examples supplied from Scripture and elsewhere are used to show that God delivers his faithful from these dilemmas. The implication (seldom, if ever, stated) is that there are no real, unavoidable moral dilemmas.

Daniel is often used as a prime example. The pagan king commanded that Daniel violate the law of God by partaking of forbidden meat and wine. But Daniel proposed "a third alternative" of vegetables and water, which God blessed and which thus brought him into the king's favor (Dan. 1).

It is said also that Sarah followed God's law and obeyed her husband's command, trusting that God would intervene and save her from having to commit adultery. This God did (Gen. 20). Of the many biblical examples where God did not intervene, it is implied that He would have intervened if the believer would have asked in faith for the deliverance, since "God is faithful; he will not let you be tempted beyond what you can bear. . . ." (I Cor. 10:13). Those who admit there are some cases in which God does not intervene claim this is because there was antecedent sin in the person's life which brought the dilemma on himself. For example, someone driving too fast might have to choose between hitting a school bus or hitting a pedestrian when there is no way between or around them. But the dilemma arises from the driver's own evil choice (fast driving). In short, sometimes we make our own moral "bed" and we have to lie in it. But many of God's people do (and all could) manifest the kind of faithfulness that says, "I will tell the truth and leave the consequences to God." A case in point occurs in Corrie Ten Boom's book, when the Ten Boom family told the truth to the Nazis. They said the Jews were hiding "under the table," but the Nazis did not see the fugitives because they were under the floor under the table. This, say some unqualified absolutists, is the sort of protection God will give if we trust Him and never lie. Hence, there is never a need to lie (or break any moral law) in order to save a life (or do any other moral good).

An Evaluation of Unqualified Absolutism

Obviously, there is much to be commended in this position, including: (1) its biblical orientation; (2) its attempt to maintain moral absolutes; (3) its grappling with difficult moral situations; (4) its search for "third alternatives"; and (5) its strong belief in the providence of God. However, the position as a whole has some serious difficulties to which we must draw attention. Since not all unqualified absolutists hold identical views, not all of these criticisms are applicable to all proponents. However, many of them will apply to all forms of the position.

Some Challengeable (or False) Premises

In this first category of criticisms fall presuppositions that are either unnecessarily or unjustifiably held by the proponents.

Are sins of the soul greater than those of the body? This platonic premise held by Augustine has by no means experienced a universal demise. Many Christians to date hold a dualistic hierarchy of this variety. This dualism has led, not without justification, to the charge that such Christians neglect social concern because they are more interested in saving souls than helping bodies. The biblical teaching on the unity of man is the corrective to this false dichotomy.[20]

---

20. See George Ladd, *The Pattern of New Testament Truth*, (Grand Rapids: Eerdmans, 1968), pp. 13-40.

If Augustine were correct in this ethical dualism, then a "white lie" or minor "evil thought" would be worse than rape or murder, for any spiritual offense would be worse than a physical one. Furthermore, Augustine was not consistent in applying this principle. Otherwise he would not have rejected the view that David should have killed Nabal (the body) in order to keep his oath (the soul).[21]

Can one separate Rahab's and the midwives' mercy and their lies? Augustine says that God blessed the mercy but not the lie. However, it was by means of the lie that the mercy was expressed and the spies were saved. There was no actual separation between the lie and the act of mercy. And a mere formal distinction will not suffice as an explanation, since in actuality there was only one act (which included the lie) under consideration, and this act was praised by God.

Are acts as such intrinsically good? Augustine argued that some acts are intrinsically good, apart from one's intentions or motives. If this is so, then theft or lying would indeed be always wrong. However, there are several reasons for rejecting the view that these acts as such are intrinsically good. First, if this were true, then an act of killing committed by an animal or an imbecile would have to be considered morally wrong. It will not suffice to add that only *human* acts of killing could be morally wrong, or else we would have to deny imbeciles are human, since they are not morally culpable for their acts. Also, adding "human" means that they were wrong because they were intended by someone, which is tantamount to saying that the act *as such* is not evil, but only the act *as intended.*

This leads to the next criticism. Augustine defined a lie,

---

21. Augustine, *Against Lying,* 9. 22.

not as a falsehood, but as an intentional falsehood. But if intention needs to be added to the act of falsifying in order to make it a lie, then it follows that the act of falsifying as such is not a lie. Further, if acts as such (for example, lying) are intrinsically evil apart from intentions or motives, then any falsification or action contrary to moral prescription in Scripture would be an evil. This would include unintentional falsehoods as well as accidental injury (or death) inflicted on persons. But to borrow Augustine's own way of speaking, everyone understands that this is not so. Finally, Augustine admitted that not all acts are intrinsically good or evil as such (for example, giving to the poor). If so, then he has already qualified his absolutism; perhaps the other acts (such as lying) are not intrinsically evil, either.

Does lying destroy all certainty? Augustine argued that lying would destroy all certainty. At best, this argument only proves that lying undermines some certainty, namely, that information based on the testimony of one known to have lied. Furthermore, the same argument could be made against anyone known to have made unintentional mistakes, which we all do. So Augustine's argument would prove too much. It would prove that one cannot be certain of anything that depends on any person. But his own Christian beliefs depended on the testimony of the apostles, which Augustine did not consider uncertain.

Is the choice between permission and commission? Nonqualified absolutists would have us believe there is no moral dilemma in the choice of lying to save a life. They believe there is really only one moral obligation for me in this situation, namely, to tell the truth. The only other duty, they say, belongs to the person threatening to do the killing. His duty is to use that truth not to kill an innocent person. But is this so? Is there not also a duty upon me to save innocent lives (that is, to show mercy)? Is there not, then, a real conflict between truth-telling and mercy-showing? In other words, the choice is really between an act of commission and one of omission. And would not a sin of omission be just as much a sin as a sin of commission?

Does lying condemn men to hell? Few Christians, Catholic or Protestant, really believe that a single lie (even a few lies scattered through one's life) are sufficient to send someone to hell. Indeed, anyone who believes in salvation by grace alone, as the Scriptures teach (Eph. 2:8, 9), will not trouble himself long with this point. It is only those whose lives are characterized by untruthfulness that eventuate in the lake of fire (Rev. 21:8). And these unsaved find themselves right alongside those who are "fearful." Yet who would say that everyone who has ever (or even occasionally) been fearful will be in hell?

Will God always save the faithful from moral dilemmas? There are several reasons to suppose that divine intervention is not the solution to all moral dilemmas. First, nowhere does the Scripture promise this to every faithful believer all the time (I Cor. 10:13 is only a promise for the victory in temptation—not a guarantee of intervention to avoid moral conflicts). Second, neither Scripture nor history supports the position that God always delivers the faithful from moral conflicts. God did deliver Daniel and Sarah, but he did not deliver the midwives, Rahab, (Josh. 2), the three Hebrew children (Dan 3), the apostles (Acts 4), or Abraham (Gen. 22). And yet the conflicts were just as real and the believers were just as faithful in these cases.

Further, not all real moral conflicts are brought on by a person's prior sin(s). Jesus seemed to face real conflicts between obeying His heavenly Father and His earthly parents (Luke 2), between mercy and sabbath-keeping (Mark 2:27), and even between justice and mercy on the cross; yet He was without sin. In fact, often moral conflicts are actually brought on by one's faithfulness to God. This was so of the midwives, of Daniel (ch. 3), of Abraham (Gen. 22), of the apostles (Acts 4–5), and even of Corrie Ten Boom. If she had not cared so much about those innocent Jews she would never have found herself in the dilemma of needing to lie to save their lives.

Was Abraham's concealment a lie? Augustine insisted that Abraham's concealment of Sarah's identity as his wife was not a lie, since she was really his (half) sister. But what about Isaac, who also claimed his wife (Rebekah) was his sister, though she was not (Gen. 26:7)? Surely this was a lie with a view to saving a life. Augustine does not address this problem.

While one can agree with Murray that there is not always an obligation to tell the whole truth (as we have in the divinely approved case of Samuel's half-truth, I Sam. 16), nonetheless, concealment sometimes is a lie. If one knows exactly what the questioner wants and yet conceals the information by intentionally misleading him, (though without direct falsification) is this not tantamount to a lie? In short, is not an intentional deception of this kind a lie?

Death by Qualification

Unqualified absolutism does not need a thousand qualifications to kill it; it can die "a death by one qualification." Any one exception to a rule proves the rule is not genuinely absolute by the unqualified absolutist's own definition of an absolute rule. And yet there are many ways the proponents of unqualified absolutism have qualified their view or made exceptions to it.

Augustine's Exceptions

Augustine admitted many exceptions to divine commands. He excused Abraham from the charge of intending to murder Isaac because Abraham was going to sacrifice his son "in obedience to God." Likewise, Jephthah's sacrifice of his daughter and Samson's sacrifice of his own life are "excused on the grounds that the Spirit of the Lord, who wrought miracles through [them], had bidden [them] to do it."[22] But even one exception kills a universal rule (as unqualified absolutists understand it); that is, it shows it not to be genuinely universally binding without exception. Likewise, Augustine argues that there were exceptions to the divine command to obey human government. It should be noted that the Bible enjoins not only submission to the consequences of a law (for example, going to prison for disobedience, Dan. 6), but it also demands obedience to the rules of government (I Peter 2:13, 14). Paul enjoins both submission and obedience, saying, "Remind the people to be subject to rulers and authorities, to be obedient . . ." (Titus 3:1, NIV).

John Murray's Qualification

Murray contended that an intentional deception is not a lie. He claims it is a "false assumption [to hold that] to be truthful we must under all circumstances speak and act in terms of the data which come within the purview of others who may be concerned with or affected by our speaking or acting."[23] But once this qualification is made one is faced with two momentous problems. First, how does he keep from allowing a thousand similar qualifications? At least Augustine limited the allowable instances of intentional deceptions to special cases involving supernatural intervention; Murray leaves the door wide open

---

22. Augustine, *City of God*, 1. 21.
23. Murray, *Principles*, p. 145.

to all kinds! Second, if a lie by definition is an intentional deception (as Augustine said), then Murray is playing ball in another park, since he no longer defines a lie in the same way. But if one allows Murray this new definition of a lie, then Murray is no longer an unqualified absolutist in the original (Augustinian) sense. What is more, Murray by virtue of his redefinitional move, is subject to the criticism that he salvages "unqualified absolutism" by stipulative redefinition. But is this really fair? Would it not be more honest to admit that there are actually times when one believes that a lie (that is, an intentional deception) is justified, rather than to redefine a lie to avoid admitting that lies are sometimes justified?

Hodge's Limitation

Charles Hodge performs another maneuver in order to rescue Augustinian absolutism from collapse. He suggests there are limitations on what counts as a lie. These limits are contextual. That is, an intentional deception counts as a lie if and only if it is told in *a context in which the truth is expected.* Since one does not expect a spy to tell the truth, it would follow that "lying" in spying is not really lying.

Several serious problems emerge from Hodge's qualification of a lie. First, it, too, suffers death by qualification. That is, it is an admission that there are exceptions to the moral rule, "Thou shalt not intentionally falsify," which is what was originally meant by a lie (in Augustine). Second, one does not expect the truth from a liar. Does this mean that a liar is not really lying when he lies as long as one knows he is a liar? This is absurd.

Some Final Observations

There are several criticisms of unqualified absolutism which emerge from the foregoing discussion which should be listed, along with some additional comments.

Note that "unqualified absolutists" are not really unqualified absolutists. They all seem to find some way to qualify divine commands. They reduce certain divine commands to less than an absolute level (a) by insisting that they flow only from God's will, not from His nature (as in Hodge); or (b) by saying some are purely civil or ceremonial in nature, not moral (as in Walter Kaiser); or (c) by claiming that the command applies only *ceterus paribus*, "all things being equal."[24]

Several things are significant in this regard. First, not all command-conflicts in Scripture can be so handled. Second, the whole division of commands into civil, ceremonial, and moral is post-biblical, questionable, and probably of late Christian origin (possibly the thirteenth century). Third, such a move to subordinate some commands to others is really not an unqualified absolutism but is actually a form of graded absolutism or hierarchicalism (see chap. 5). Finally, many subordinations or qualifications of any kind is a capitulation of *unqualified* absolutism, since it admits there are occasions when moral commands must be qualified.

As a matter of fact, God does not intervene and spare all the faithful from moral dilemmas. There is no evidence for this premise of unqualified absolutism either inside or outside the Bible. Indeed, the premise of supernatural intervention is in conflict with other premises held by these absolutists.

To begin with, why the need for intervention if all conflicts are only apparent and not real? The need for divine intervention is a concession to the truth (which is contrary to the tenets of unqualifed absolutism) that there are real conflicts. For once one admits that there are real moral conflicts and that they can be resolved by divine in-

---

24. See Walter Kaiser, "Legitimate Hermeneutics," in *Inerrancy*, ed. Norman L. Geisler (Grand Rapids: Zondervan, 1980), chap. 5.

tervention, then he is no longer an unqualified absolutist but is some kind of hierarchicalist or graded absolutist.

Further, why the need for intervention if all moral dilemmas are caused by antecedent sin? God may sometimes in His mercy desire to intervene, but there is no reason to believe He must (or will) always do so.

We should not always expect miracles to help us out of real moral conflicts. Many unqualified absolutists "solve" the ethical dilemma problem with recourse to the belief that God will always spare the faithful. This, however, meets with several serious objections.

(1) First of all, God nowhere promises that He will always intervene.

(2) The three Hebrew children did not expect God to bail them out of their moral dilemma (Dan. 3).

(3) Jesus spoke against expecting a miracle to get one out of difficult situations (Matt. 4:7).

(4) Expecting a miracle shifts the responsibility from us to God. It is a kind of "if in trouble, punt to God" ethic.

(5) We ought not base the reality of a present decision on the possibility that God may perform a miracle in the future.

(6) Believing that God will intervene if we do "right" begs the question. It assumes that there is always a way to do right without real moral conflict.

(7) Such a view would demand frequent miraculous intervention. But frequent miraculous intervention would make life and miracles impossible, since both depend on regular patterns of activity for their operation.

(8) Finally, there are some pertinent questions to answer if one trusts God to intervene. In the scenerio of the Christian called upon to reveal the whereabouts of an innocent victim to a would-be assassin, why not trust God to intervene before one speaks the truth (by creating dumbness)? That way the hiding place of the innocent is not disclosed. Or why not trust God to intervene and cause deafness in the would-be assassin, or the like?

Further, antecedent personal sin does not cause all moral dilemmas. Even if one insists that Adam's antecedent sin is the ultimate course of all subsequent moral dilemmas, this is nevertheless not true personally. That is, not every individual brings on his own moral dilemmas by personal antecedent sins.[25] If the sense in which it is said that we all sinned antecedently "in Adam" were the cause of all ethical actions, then we are all sinning all the time in all that we do. But to argue this way would be to confuse depravity and ethical responsibility, and it would leave no explanation why any action at any time should be considered good. At best, personal antecedent sins cause only some of one's personal moral conflicts. Some are caused by others who force the conflict on the innocent. Indeed, sometimes just the opposite is true, namely, personal moral dilemmas are precipitated by one's faithfulness or righteousness.

Note that most (if not virtually all) unqualified absolutists are inconsistent. They engage in intentional deception of various kinds with self-approval and yet condemn lying to save a life. Most people, for example, leave their lights on while away from home in order to deceive potential thieves. But if one will lie to save his property from a potential thief, then why not lie to save an innocent life from an actual murderer?

Another problem is that the unqualified absolutist often ends up committing unmerciful acts. He performs greater sins of omission in order to avoid what he believes to be sins of commission. Plato's example (Republic, I. 330) is instructive. Who would return a weapon he had borrowed from a man if the man requested it in order to kill someone with it? The law of mercy is higher than the law

---

25. There is of course the virtual, or seminal sense (some would say, legal), in which all men sinned in Adam (Rom. 5:12). But this was not a personal sin, since we did not preexist as persons in Adam.

of property rights. Likewise, the Scriptures seem to indicate that life-saving of the innocent (mercy) is a greater duty than truth-telling to the guilty (Exod. 1).

Also, unqualified absolutism often tends to legalism by neglecting the spirit of the law in order to avoid breaking the letter of the law. This is precisely what Jesus condemned when he said, "The sabbath was made for man, not man for the sabbath" (Mark 2:27). Is not the unqualified absolutist violating the spirit of the law when he does not give the Nazi interrogator the truth for which he is asking but only part of it? His intent is to mislead him (such as in the illustration from the Ten Booms' experience of hiding the Jews under the table).

Finally, silence and other "third alternatives" are not always possible. Samuel was saved from Saul's wrath by revealing only one of his two purposes in coming to Bethlehem (I Sam. 16:2). But what if Saul had asked him what other mission he had in mind? At that point he would have had to either lie, be silent (which would have implied he had another purpose for coming), or else risk the death of the innocent (namely, be unmerciful). Even silence before an interrogator who says, "I will kill X unless you speak" can be an unmerciful sin of omission.

Conclusion

Despite the many desirable aspects of unqualified absolutism, and its noble efforts to preserve unmodified absolutes, the efforts are unsuccessful. In short, it is unrealistic, unmerciful (even legalistic at times), and unsuccessful in avoiding the inevitable modification of its absolutes in order to give an adequate answer to numerous biblical and real-life conflicts of divine commands. It is no doubt ideally correct in the sense that God does not design nor desire moral conflicts. But this is not an ideal world; it is a real and fallen world. And if the Christian ethic is adequate for the world in which we live, then it must not retreat into unqualified absolutes. It must find a morally excellent way to preserve absolutes and yet honestly and adequately provide an answer for every moral situation.

Chapter **4**

Option Two:

Conflicting Absolutism

Evangelicals have generally held to some form of ethical absolutism. In contrast to situationism, they have claimed that there are many moral absolutes. Within the camp of those holding to two or more absolutes, a special problem arises: What about moral conflicts?[1] That is, what ought one do when two or more of his absolute obligations come into unavoidable conflict?

Basically, there are three answers to this question.[2] First, unqualified absolutists affirm that all such conflicts

---

1. It is lamentable that Carl Henry does not discuss the problem of moral conflicts anywhere in his two volumes on ethics. See *Aspects of Christian Social Ethics* (Grand Rapids: Eerdmans, 1964), and *Christian Personal Ethics* (Grand Rapids: Eerdmans, 1957). Edward J. Carnell, *Christian Commitment* (Grand Rapids: Eerdmans, 1957), gave seven pages to the topic (pp. 223-29).

2. Elsewhere *(Ethics: Alternatives and Issues,* [Grand Rapids: Zondervan, 1971], chapters 2, 3, 4) we have called these three views, respectively, non-conflicting absolutism, ideal absolutism, and hierarchicalism. In popular language I call them "third alternative, lesser-evil, and greater-good views *(The Christian Ethic of Love,* [Grand Rapids: Zondervan, 1973]).

67

are only apparent; they are not real. In short, no two absolute obligations ever come into unavoidable conflict. Second, conflicting absolutism (or the lesser-evil view) admits to real moral conflicts but claims that one is guilty no matter which way he goes. Third, graded absolutism (or the greater-good position) agrees with the lesser-evil view that real moral conflicts do sometimes occur, but maintains that one is personally guiltless if he does the greatest good in that situation. This chapter will consider the second view.

The Basis of Conflicting Absolutism

The central assumption of the ethical position of conflicting absolutism is that we live in a fallen world, and in such a world real moral conflicts do occur. The accompanying premise is, however, that when two duties conflict, man is morally responsible to both duties. God's law can never be broken without guilt. In such cases, therefore, one must simply do the lesser evil, confess his sin, and ask for God's forgiveness.

An Absolutely Perfect Law of God

There are three central principles in conflicting absolutism. First, God's law is absolutely perfect. "The law of the Lord is perfect" (Ps. 19:7). The psalmist confessed to God, "Every one of thy righteous ordinances endures for ever" (119:160). God has not made His law to be broken. The psalmist exclaimed, "Thou [God] hast commanded thy precepts to be kept diligently" (Ps. 119:4). "The judgments of the Lord are true and righteous altogether"; and "in keeping of them there is great reward" (Ps. 19:9, 11). Further, "Jehovah will not hold him guiltless" who breaks His commands (Exod. 20:7, ASV).

In short, God is absolutely perfect and His law is a

reflection of His character. "You, therefore must be perfect, as your heavenly Father is perfect" (Matt. 5:48). Anything that does not measure up to the absolute perfection of the law of God is sin. Whenever God's law is broken, the lawbreaker sins, for "sin is lawlessness" (I John 3:4).

A Sinful World

The second premise of conflicting absolutism is the depravity of man. Man has broken God's law and finds himself inextricably enmeshed in a web of sinful relationships in which sin is unavoidable. He is fallen by nature and, hence, must sin.[3] Before the fall of man, Adam was able not to sin, but since the fall, man is unable to avoid sin. Did not Jesus say, "It is necessary that temptations come" (Matt. 18:7)? Men are "by nature children of wrath" (Eph. 2:3).

Not only can man not avoid sinning in general, but there are tragic moral dilemmas in this fallen world in which *all* alternatives are wrong. No matter what one does, he cannot avoid breaking one of God's laws. That is the reality of a fallen world. Sometimes one must sin. He must, of course, choose the lesser evil, but he must sin, regardless.

Conflicting absolutism runs contrary to the Kantian dictum that "ought implies can."[4] Man is always called upon to obey a standard of perfection he cannot reach (for example, "You, therefore, must be perfect, as your heavenly Father is perfect" [Matt. 5:48]). Further, in moral dilemmas one is morally obligated to keep both laws, even though one of them must be broken. Such it is in this sinful

---

3. The unavoidability of sin follows, according to conflicting absolutists, from the doctrine of depravity. See Carl Henry, *Christian Personal Ethics*, pp. 168, 393.

4. Henry, ibid., says, "the formula, 'I ought, but I cannot,' summarizes the predicament of fallen and unregenerate man."

world, says the conflicting absolutist. Ideally, God did not design it this way. But then again, this wicked world is far from ideal.

Forgiveness Is Available

The third premise associated with conflicting absolutism is that even though sin is sometimes unavoidable, God's forgiveness is always available through the cross of Christ. Indeed, one of the happy by-products of this sad world is that the unavoidability of sin drives men to the cross for forgiveness.[5] There is a "way out" of the dilemma. It is not a way to avoid sin; sin is unavoidable by the nature of the case. Rather, it is a way to avoid bearing long the guilt of the sin. In brief, the way out is, on our part, confession and, on God's part, the sacrifice of Christ on the cross. All one need do in lesser-evil situations is to do the lesser evil, confess that he has broken God's law, and receive forgiveness through Jesus Christ. Sin is unavoidable, but salvation is available.

An Evaluation of Conflicting Absolutism

A number of objections have been leveled against the lesser-evil view. We will consider four of them here. The first two may be called moral and the last two christological. First, it has been argued that it is morally absurd to say one is morally obligated to do evil. How can there ever be a *moral* obligation to do what is immoral?

The Painful Alternatives

There are three basic alternatives for the proponent of the lesser-evil position in view of this criticism. First, he might claim that there is no moral obligation (that is,

5. This point was made by John W. Montgomery in his debate with Joseph Fletcher. See *Situation Ethics* (Minneapolis: Bethany Fellowship, 1972), pp. 46, 68.

divine command) to do the lesser evil. It is simply what one "ought" to do, on some kind of pragmatic or utilitarian grounds, for personal or social reasons. This alternative would seem to be particularly embarrassing for the biblical Christian, since he would be faced with some of life's most difficult situations without any direction or command from God. Christianity would have an incomplete ethic. It would be able to handle the ordinary situations, but for the really difficult ones—the ones involving tragic moral choices—it would give absolutely no divine direction.

There is another way out of the dilemma for the lesser-evil proponent. He may admit that there is a moral obligation, not to do evil, but simply to maximize good (or minimize evil) in an evil situation. But if he takes this route, then his position really collapses into the greater-good view. For if he is actually obligated to do a maximal good, then why call it evil?[6] For example, the doctor who amputates a patient's leg to save his life is not guilty of the sin of mutilation, but is to be commended for doing the maximal good. Surely, as tragic as amputation is, there is no basis in Christian ethics to consider amputation done to save a life as a culpable act. Likewise, why call the act evil, as the lesser-evil view would seem to do, when it was the greatest good under the circumstances?

Finally, of course, the lesser-evil view could simply admit the absurdity and unavoidability of sin and claim that one is morally obligated to do what is morally wrong, absurd as this is.

Guilt for the Unavoidable

This leads to a second criticism, that the lesser-evil view holds that one is personally responsible for what is

---

6. For a good contemporary work dedicated to this thesis see *Doing Evil to Achieve Good: Moral Choice in Conflict Situations*, ed. R. McCormick and P. Ramsey (Chicago: Loyola University Press, 1978).

personally unavoidable. Those who espouse the lesser-evil view challenge the underlying premise of their opponents that responsibility implies ability, that ought implies can. They may point to biblical instances where God commands the impossible, such as, "Be perfect, as your heavenly Father is perfect" (Matt. 5:48). They may point to the doctrine of depravity which declares it impossible for a man not to sin though God commands a man not to sin.

But in these cases one need simply note that "ought implies can" only in the sense that one "can," by the enabling grace of God, do what is utterly impossible by human standards. In this sense, the "ought implies can" thesis is not a violation of these biblical truths. Furthermore, to focus on the "ought implies can" principle misses the real issue. The moral absurdity of the lesser-evil position is not based on the truth or falsity of "ought implies can." From a Christian standpoint it is morally absurd to say "one ought to do an evil," since "ought" means "God has commanded it"; and God does not (I would say, *cannot*) command one to do what is morally evil. God is good, absolute good, and as such He can neither perform nor promote that which is evil. For God to command one to do evil would contradict His very will (I would say, *nature*).

Of course, one might respond here by claiming that whatever God commands is *ipso facto* good and not evil, since one could define good as that which God commands. However, this response would be fatal to the lesser-evil view. For if what God commands in so-called lesser-evil situations is really good (simply because He commanded it), then it is not an evil. In fact, if the act is good in this conflicting situation because God commanded it, then the lesser-evil view has really collapsed into the greater-good view. For the good act one is performing at the command of God is not sinful but commendable, because it is done in obedience to God.

Before we leave this point, it should be noted that making a distinction between good and right does not help the lesser-evil position.[7] One cannot simply claim that the "lesser-evil" act is simply the "right" thing to do in that situation. For one can always ask the question: Was the "right act" morally good or evil? That is, was the act culpable or not? If it is morally evil or guilt-inducing, then we are right back where we started and the above criticisms apply. If, on the other hand, the "right act" was good or guiltless, then the view has collapsed into the greater-good view.

The essential difference between these two positions is that according to the lesser-evil view the tragic moral act is guilt-inducing and calls for confession and forgiveness, whereas according to the greater-good view the tragic moral act is guiltless. One may regret having to make the decision, but he need not repent of it. Indeed, according to the greater-good view, doing the greatest good leads to reward—not to punishment. At any rate, the lesser-evil view is not redeemed from its difficulties by calling the "lesser-evil" act the "right" act in contrast to a "good" act. The question still remains: Is one personally guilty or not for performing this act? If guilty, then God is commanding an act which is unavoidably sinful. If not guilty, then the act is morally acceptable and we are driven to the greater-good position.

There is another distinction sometimes made in an attempt to rescue the lesser-evil position. It is occasionally claimed that one is not blamed *for* doing his best in conflicting situations, but rather he is blamed *in* doing his best. For even the most faithful servant is unworthy (Luke

---

7. For this distinction see Millard J. Erickson, *Relativism in Contemporary Ethics*, (Grand Rapids: Baker Book House, 1974), pp. 41, 118, 143. H. P. Owen criticizes this distinction in *The Moral Argument for Christian Theism* (New York: Humanities Press, 1965), chapter 1.

17:10). In this sense it might be claimed that it would be morally absurd to blame one for doing his best, but it is not necessarily absurd to blame one for doing evil *in the process of* doing his best. Might it not be that the act of lying is evil but the whole process of mercy-showing to the innocent is the greatest good? Hence, one should confess the lie in particular even though the act *as a whole* was the greatest good. Perhaps God blames a man for whatever sinful acts are part of an overall good performance.

In response to this distinction, we might simply note that the ethical complex must be thought of as a whole. For certain things done in one context are morally good and in another are morally evil. For example, cutting off a man's leg is good if done by a doctor as a necessary means to save a life, but evil if done as an act of sadism. It is the moral context as a whole that gives meaning to the act. Hence, one cannot separate specific evil parts from an overall ethical performance and call the whole act good. Amputation as an intention-act complex is either good or evil. One cannot claim that the overall amputation process was good but the actual cutting of a human leg was evil.

This discussion brings up a more principal issue beneath the whole discussion, specifically, the relation of intention to action in judging the morality of an act. It appears that the difficulty with much of the discussion on these issues hinges on the question of whether an act is intrinsically good or evil or whether it is the intention-act complex that must be considered. An adequate discussion of this is beyond the scope of this volume. Suffice it to say here that it seems most reasonable to assume that the latter is the case. Good intentions alone are not sufficient to make an act morally right. Hitler may have intended to produce a better world by attempting genocide, but the murder of millions of Jews was not made morally good by admirable motives. Likewise, an act as such apart from its motive or intention is not necessarily good. For instance, those who give to the poor in order to receive the praise of men are not to be morally commended. If this is the case, then the lesser-evil position is wrong to separate an act from its total intention-act complex and pronounce it evil and declare the overall process good.

The Christological Problem

We turn now to the third criticism of the lesser-evil position and to some possible responses. The third flaw involves a christological problem. If there are real moral dilemmas, then either Jesus faced them or else He did not. If He did, then according to the lesser-evil view which states that evil is indeed unavoidable, Jesus must have sinned. But the Bible says Jesus did not sin (Heb. 4:15; II Cor. 5:21). Hence, the only alternative here is that He never faced real moral conflicts. Assuming there are real moral conflicts, several explanations for this dilemma can be offered. First, perhaps the lesser-evil view is incorrect, and Jesus never sinned when He faced real moral conflicts because one is not held sinful when he does the greatest good in a moral conflict. Perhaps "stealing" bread from the temple (that is, taking it without permission of the proper authority) is not morally wrong when starvation of God's servant is the other alternative. Is this not what Jesus implied in Matthew 12?

But let us not so readily assume that the lesser-evil position is defenseless. It may be that Jesus never sinned in the area of moral conflicts simply because He never faced any. There are two explanations for this position. First, it may be that God providentially spared Jesus from facing lesser-evil situations in order to preserve His sinlessness. But if this is the case, then the Christian may ask why he, too, is not spared from them if he is faithful to God. In fact, this is precisely what many non-conflicting absolutists hold, specifically, that there is always a third alternative for the faithful. Daniel did not have either to eat the pagan meat and drink the pagan wine or suffer the consequence of his disobedience (Dan. 1). There was a prayerful third way out. Is this not what I Corinthians 10:13 seems to imply, that there is "always a way of escape?" If the lesser-evil view wishes to take this alternative of arguing that God will always provide a way out for those who are faithful to God's will, as Jesus was, then their view really collapses into non-conflicting absolutism. For, in the final analysis, the lesser-evil view is saying there is no unavoidable moral conflict for those who do God's will.[8] It would be special pleading to declare that the providential way out applies only to Christ but not to other servants of God who are faithful to His will.

A more plausible suggestion is that Jesus never faced any moral dilemmas simply because He never committed any antecedent sin to get Himself into these tight spots.[9] Only those who make their moral "beds" have to lie in them. Jesus never sinned and, hence, He never found Himself in unavoidable moral conflicts. On the face of it, this view has merit. It does seem to be often the case that our previous sins get us into a moral "pickle." We do reap what we sow. However, in order for this obvious truth to rescue the lesser-evil position from collapse it must be universally true. That is, it must always be the case that moral dilemmas we face are created by our own antecedent sins. However, this seems patently false by counter example. Sometimes it is the innocent who are faced with moral difficulties. What sin did innocent German Christian families commit that placed them in the dilemma of either lying or watching Jews go to the gas chamber?

---

8. Unqualified absolutism has already been discussed and critiqued in chapter 3.

9. This view was suggested by Erwin Lutzer, *The Morality Gap* (Chicago: Moody Press, 1972), pp. 111-12.

Were these believers more sinful than others in the world? One is reminded here of Jesus' statement about those on whom the tower fell: "Do you think that they were worse offenders than all the others who dwelt in Jerusalem? (Luke 13:4).

Indeed, not only is it not true that moral dilemmas are always brought about by antecedent sin, but sometimes it is antecedent righteousness that precipitates the dilemma. Daniel and the three Hebrew children were not confronted with their dilemma because they were backslidden (cf. Dan. 1, 3, 6). Nor were the apostles doing evil when they were commanded not to preach, thus forcing a choice between the command to obey government and the command to preach the gospel (Acts 4). The same is true of Abraham's dilemma as to whether to kill his son or to disobey God (Gen. 22). Indeed, many times in life it is one's dedication to God that precipitates moral conflicts. That is, it is his righteousness, not his antecedent sin, that occasions the moral conflict. If this is the case, then the lesser-evil position has not redeemed itself against the criticisms. It has not explained away the christological dilemma. It has not shown that Jesus never faced moral dilemmas simply because He never committed any previous sins.

Before the opponents of the lesser-evil view rejoice too quickly, there is another point to consider. Perhaps there is always antecedent sin in our case, but never in Christ's case—because we are fallen but He is not. Adam's sin is antecedent in the case of all men except Christ. Hence, because we are part of a fallen world, previous sin (that is, Adam's, see Rom. 5:12) is responsible for subsequent moral dilemmas we will face but Christ did not.

There is a certain plausibility about this suggestion that cannot be denied. It would seem to point to a clear difference in Christ's case, as well as to recognize antecedent sin in our case. There are, however, at least two problems here. First, moral conflicts due to antecedent sin of Adam are not unique to fallen man; Christ also lived in this fallen world. And even though He never personally sinned, Christ was nevertheless immersed in a world of moral conflicts due to Adam's and others' sins. It must be remembered that not all moral conflicts are due to one's own antecedent sin. The sins of others can force a dilemma on those who did not personally create the tragic situation. The question would then be, Why did not Christ face any moral conflicts forced on Him by the sins of others?

Second, the attempt to explain why Christ did not face moral conflicts by way of Adam's fall confuses collective and personal guilt. There is a corporate sense in which everything done by fallen man is sinful. Even the plowing of the wicked man is sin (Prov. 21:4). In this sense, sin is inevitable for all fallen men. This, however, is quite different from saying that a man is personally guilty for creating the situation, or that any particular sin is unavoidable. The immediate moral choice may not induce guilt because it is unavoidable. However, were it not for Adam's fall, that kind of situation would never have occurred. For example, one would never have to kill in self-defense were it not for Adam's fall (there would, presumably, be no need to kill for any reason in a paradise). Nonetheless, killing in self-defense is not a personally culpable act according to the law of God (Exod. 22:2).

We may still ask: Did Jesus really face moral dilemmas in which two or more commands of God came into unavoidable conflict? An examination of the Gospels yields several illustrations: At age twelve Jesus faced a conflict between His earthly parents and His heavenly Father. Although He later submitted to his earthly parents, initially He left them in order to fulfill God's will (Luke 2). It is parenthetically noteworthy in this context that Jesus justified His disciples' action of taking grain by approving

David's "stealing" of the shewbread in the tabernacle (Matt. 12:3f.). In this regard Jesus said to others, "He who loves father or mother more than me is not worthy of me" (Matt. 10:37). On many occasions Jesus faced conflict between obeying the religious authorities (which He Himself taught His disciples and others to do, Matt. 23:2), and following the law of mercy by helping those in need (Luke 14:1-6). For example, He chose to heal a man on the Sabbath. When challenged He said the law of the Sabbath should be subordinated to man; not vice versa. On another occasion Jesus approved of the disciples plucking grain on the Sabbath (Luke 6:1-5).

The greatest moral conflict that Jesus faced, however, was His trial and cross, where mercy and justice came into direct and unavoidable conflict. Should He speak in defense of the innocent (Himself) as the law demanded (Lev. 5:1), or should He show mercy to the many (mankind)? Further, should He take His own life in a self-sacrifice for others (cf. John 10:10), or should He refuse to die unjustly for others? In both cases Jesus chose mercy over justice. But did He sin in so doing? God forbid! The cross was not the lesser of two evils; it was the greatest good ("greater love hath no man . . ."). It appears that the lesser-evil view, then, literally stands at the crossroads. If it is a sin to do the greatest good in a morally conflicting situation, then Jesus would have been perhaps the greatest sinner who ever lived. Perish the thought! Indeed, God Himself faced a moral conflict in the cross: Should He sacrifice His Son or should He allow the world to perish? Thank God, mercy triumphed over justice. Surely the sacrifice of Christ was not a lesser evil; it was indeed the greatest good God could do (cf. John 15:13 and Rom. 5:8, 9).

The fourth objection is another christological problem with the lesser-evil view. If Christ is our complete moral example, then He must have faced morally conflicting situations in which both alternatives were sinful. But if Christ never sinned, then Christ never faced them. Hence, we have no example from Christ to follow in some of life's most difficult moral decisions. But does not Hebrews say He was "tempted in every way, just as we are" (4:15, NIV)? Does not Paul exhort us to "be followers of Christ" (I Cor. 11:1f., KJV)? But how can we follow Him in ethical dilemmas if He never faced them?

Some proponents of the lesser-evil view frankly admit Christ is not our complete moral example. But it is unacceptable to grant this point. It concedes that the ethic of following Christ is incomplete for the followers of Christ. Indeed, a proper understanding of the New Testament would dictate that we give up claims of the lesser-evil view rather than sacrifice the completeness of Christ's moral example.

The proof that one can face real moral dilemmas without sinning is that Jesus faced them but never sinned. If this is so, then it follows that moral dilemmas do not necessitate personal guilt. There is always "a way of escape" through doing the greater good.[10] In conflicting situations, keeping the higher law (for example, obedience to God over government) is the guiltless way out.

Conclusion

The lesser-evil view does not appear to have successfully defended itself against either the moral or the christological charges leveled against it. When pushed to the wall it seems to collapse into either non-conflicting absolutism by claiming special providential intervention, or into the greater-good view by claiming that one is morally obligated to maximize good. In short, it seems to have no firm ground of its own on which to stand.

---

10. See the next chapter for a discussion of this point.

Option Three:

Graded Absolutism

Total ethical relativism is not a genuine option for an evangelical. God's character is unchanging, and His law reflects His character (chapter 2). Of the options within ethical absolutism, evangelicals must choose between unqualified absolutism (chapter 3), conflicting absolutism (chapter 4), or graded absolutism (chapter 5). Our previous analysis, however, has indicated serious, if not insurmountable, problems with the first two of these views. There remains one alternative to discuss, namely, graded absolutism. Since this is the view espoused in this book, we will first indicate the basis on which it has been built and then proceed to answer objections which have been leveled against it.

The Basis of Graded Absolutism

For the sake of simplicity and clarity we will outline the arguments for graded absolutism and give the biblical support for each premise.[1] There are three essential

1. For further support of this point see my *Christian Ethic of Love* (Grand Rapids: Zondervan, 1973), chapters 3, 7-9.

premises in the biblical argument for graded absolutism.
Each is based on relevant Scripture.

Higher and Lower Moral Laws

Not all moral laws are of equal weight. Jesus spoke of
the "weightier" matters of the law (Matt. 23:23) and of
the "least" (Matt. 5:19) and the "greatest" commandments (Matt. 22:36). He told Pilate that Judas had committed the "greater sin" (John 19:11). Despite a rather
widespread evangelical distaste for a hierarchy of sins
(and virtues), the Bible does speak of the "greatest" virtue (I Cor. 13:13) and even of "greater" acts of a given virtue (John 15:13).

The common myth that all sins are equal is often based
on erroneous interpretations of James 2:10, which does
not speak of the equality of all sins but of the unity of law.
"He who offends in one point is guilty of all." He is not
equally guilty of all, and all infractions do not bring equal
guilt (compare James 3:1), but it is true that any violation
of the law brings some guilt. Others have supposed
wrongly that simply because Jesus said that one can lust
and even murder "in his heart" (Matt. 5:28) that this
means it is equally evil to imagine a sin as it is to do it. In
the same sermon Jesus rejected this view, indicating there
are at least three levels of sins with corresponding
judgments (5:22). Indeed, the whole concept of degrees of
punishment in hell (Matt. 5:22; Rom. 2:6; Rev. 20:12) and
graded levels of reward in heaven (I Cor. 3:11f.) indicates
that sins come in degrees. The fact that some Christian
sins called for excommunication (I Cor. 5) and others for
death (I Cor. 11:30) also supports the general biblical pattern that all sins are not equal in weight. Indeed, there is
one sin so great as to be unforgivable (Mark 3:29).

Perhaps the clearest indication of higher and lower
moral laws comes in Jesus' answer to the lawyer's question about the "greatest commandment" (Matt. 22:34ff.).

Jesus clearly affirmed that the "first" and "greatest" was over the "second," that loving God is of supreme importance, and then beneath that comes loving one's neighbor. This same point is reaffirmed when our Lord said, "He who loves father or mother more than me is not worthy of me" (Matt. 10:37). Numerous other scriptural passages can be listed to support this same point (cf. Prov. 6:16; I Tim. 1:15; I John 5:16; Matt. 5:22). The popular belief is wrong; all sins are not created equal, for there are indeed higher and lower moral laws.[2]

It is of more than passing significance to note that *both* other Christian options admit the truth of this same point. The conflicting absolutist speaks of the *lesser* evil, clearly implying that not all evils are equal.[3] Likewise, the unqualified absolutist admits that moral laws are higher than civil or ceremonial laws commanded by God, and that many laws are binding only if all things are equal, which they sometimes are not.[4] The real question, then, is, Are the moral laws hierarchically graded?

The answer is affirmative for several reasons. First, all ethical obligations are moral laws, and Christians do have an ethical obligation to obey civil laws (cf. Rom. 13:1-4; I Peter 2:13, 14). It is not simply a civil duty to obey civil laws, since such obedience is enjoined by the moral law Giver (God) for "conscience's sake" (Rom. 13:5). Second, even the commands to obey government or perform ceremonial duties are divine commands and, as such, in-

---

2. Dr. Walter Kaiser has taken a step in the right direction by admitting that there are "weightier matters of the law" (Matt. 23:23), indicating a hierarchy of divine commands. He does not, however, yet fully appreciate the moral nature of the lower commands. See his chapter "The Weightier and Lighter Matters of the Law" in *Current Issues in Biblical and Patristic Interpretation*, ed. Gerald F. Hawthorne, (Grand Rapids: Eerdmans, 1975).

3. See discussion in chapter 4.

4. See chapter 3.

volve a moral duty. By its very nature a divine command which one ought to obey is an ethical responsibility. Otherwise it would be a mere declarative or descriptive statement, not an imperative. Third, the distinctions between civil, ceremonial, and moral laws are not rigid (if maintainable at all). The law of God has unity and interpenetrability, so that there are moral implications to civil and ceremonial commands. Whatever God commands His children to do—whether love their neighbors or offer sacrifices—demands moral obedience.[5] Finally, some of the conflicts in commands are clearly between two commands which are both moral in nature, even by those who distinguish between moral and civil or ceremonial (for example, Gen. 22; Matt. 2; Exod. 1 on lying). We conclude that there are indeed graded levels of moral commands in Scripture.

Unavoidable Moral Conflicts Exist

Some personally unavoidable moral conflicts exist in which an individual cannot obey both commands. The arguments in support of this observation come from many sources—both inside and outside of the Bible. Several of them will suffice to establish this point.

First, the Abraham and Isaac story (Gen. 22) contains a real moral conflict. "Thou shalt not kill" is a divine moral command, and yet God commanded Abraham to kill his son, Isaac.[6] That Abraham intended to kill Isaac is clear

---

5. In fact, the entire concept of distinctions between moral law, civil law, and ceremonial law is questionable. No clear-cut division between these is made in Scripture, and I have not been able to trace the distinction back any farther than the thirteenth century.

6. Sören Kierkegaard's contention in *Fear and Trembling* that the religious transcends the ethical is unacceptable to an evangelical. It is based on an unjustifiable separation of the moral law Giver (God) and His moral law. It wrongly assumes that there can be a non-propositional, personal revelation to the individual which transcends all universal, rational, and propositional categories.

from the context, and from Hebrews 11, which informs us that Abraham believed God would raise Isaac from the dead (v. 19). Further, the fact that Abraham was not required to go through with the act does not eliminate the reality of the moral conflict, since the *intention* to perform an act with moral implications is itself a morally responsible act (cf. Matt. 5:28). Neither will it suffice to say that this is a specially approved divine exception, because the "exception" (or exemption) must be made in view of some higher law (or purpose) of God; this is precisely the point graded absolutism wishes to make. Furthermore, the very fact that an "exception" (or exemption) is called for indicates that the two laws are in genuine conflict.

Second, the story of Samson contains a conflict of two divine commands. Samson committed a divinely approved suicide (Judg. 16:30) despite the moral prohibition against killing (one's self). Both commands were divine and moral (first, Do not kill, and second, Take your life); yet, when there was a real conflict between them, God apparently approved of disregarding one in order to obey the other.

Third, the passage detailing Jephthah's sacrifice of his daughter (Judg. 11) shows a real moral conflict between a vow to God (which is inviolate, Eccles. 5:1-4) and the command not to kill an innocent life.[7] The usual answer of unqualified absolutists, namely, that one is not obligated to keep a vow that necessarily involves sin, will not work here. For according to that explanation, Jephthah should not have kept his vow to kill his daughter. But the Scripture appears to approve of Jephthah keeping the oath to kill.

---

7. This, of course, is built on the traditional interpretation of the passage. Recently some have suggested that Jephthah did not sacrifice his daughter's life but her marital life, making her a perpetual virgin (see Judg. 11:38). This, however, is difficult to understand in view of the vow (verse 31) in which he said, "... whatever comes out of the doors ... I will offer it up as a burnt offering" (NASB).

Fourth, there are several biblical illustrations in which individuals had to choose between lying and not helping to save a life (that is, not showing mercy). The Hebrew midwives (Exod. 1) and Rahab (Josh. 2) will suffice as examples. Regardless of whether they were right or wrong in lying, the point here is that the conflict was genuine and both obligations were moral ones. It is not sufficient to claim silence as a "third alternative," because even silence can lead to murder when deception is necessary to ward off an assassin. This is often the case, and it is unmistakably the case if the assassin says, "Either tell me the truth or I will kill X." It will not do to claim that there is no real conflict in these cases on the grounds that in telling the truth the midwives would not be murdering the babies (Pharaoh would). For in the very act of telling the truth, the midwives would be unmerciful. In other words, to avoid what they believed to be the lesser sin of commission (lying), they would be engaging in a greater sin of omission (not showing mercy).

Fifth, there is a real moral conflict in the cross, one so great that many liberal theologians have considered the doctrine of the substitutionary atonement as essentially immoral. The two moral principles are: (1) the innocent should not be punished for sins he never committed (Ezek. 18:20), and yet (2) Christ was punished for our sins (Isa. 53; I Peter 2:24; 3:18; II Cor. 5:21). Some have tried to solve the problem by suggesting that Christ submitted to this punishment voluntarily, and hence the moral responsibility for the conflict disappears.[8] But this is like saying it was not immoral for Rev. Jim Jones to order the Jamestown suicide because his followers did it willingly! Other attempted explanations make God's actions in the cross entirely arbitrary, with no necessary basis in His

---

8. This view is called *voluntarism* and has been critiqued earlier (see chapter 1 under "Relativism in the Middle Ages").

unchanging moral character. But this reduces God to an
unworthy being, and takes away the need for the cross.
For if God could save men apart from the cross, then
Christ's death becomes unnecessary.

Sixth, there are numerous cases in Scripture in which
there is a real conflict between obeying God's command
to submit to civil government and keeping one's duty to
some other (higher) moral law. For example, the Hebrew
midwives disregarded Pharaoh's command to kill all male
infants (Exod. 1); the Jewish captives disregarded Neb-
uchadnezzar's command to worship the golden image of
himself (Dan. 3); Daniel disregarded Darius's command to
pray only to the king (Dan. 6). In each case there was
plainly no other alternative; those involved had to follow
one or the other of the two commandments. Even the unqualified absolutist admits the unavoidability of the conflict, since he reduces one command (the civil one) to a
lower level. This maneuver, however, does not take away
from the fact that (1) both are commands of God with
moral implications, and (2) the situation was personally
unavoidable. That is, there was no prior sin on the part of
those in the dilemma that precipitated their dilemma. In
all these cases it was *because* they were moral, godly people that they found themselves in the dilemma.

There are many other biblical examples of genuine,
unavoidable moral conflicts, but the foregoing examples
suffice. Even one clear case of an unavoidable conflict is
enough to prove the point. We move, then, to the next
premise.

No Guilt Is Imputed to Us for the Unavoidable

God does not hold the individual responsible for personally unavoidable moral conflicts, providing they keep
the higher law. There are a number of ways of seeing the
truth of this point.

First, logic dictates that a just God will not hold a person responsible for doing what is actually impossible. And it is actually impossible to avoid the unavoidable. It is impossible to take both opposite courses of action at the same time.

Second, one is not morally culpable if he fails to keep an obligation he could not possibly keep without breaking a higher obligation. This is evident to all, even to those evangelicals who hold opposing ethical views. Clearly a person is not blameworthy for breaking a promise to meet his wife for dinner at six o'clock if he has been delayed by helping to save a life. Likewise, who would blame a man for refusing to return a gun to an angry neighbor who wants to kill his wife?[9] In each case, the praiseworthy and exemplar conduct of keeping the higher obligation alleviates one of any responsibility to the lower duty.

Third, the Bible includes many examples of persons who were praised by God for following their highest duty in conflict situations. Abraham was commended of God for his willingness to sacrifice (kill) his son Isaac for God (Gen. 22; Heb. 11). Likewise, Daniel (Dan. 6) and the three Hebrew children received divine approval for their disobedience to human government. The Hebrew midwives were blessed of God for their disobedience to the king's command (Exod. 1). David and his men who broke into the temple and stole the shewbread were declared guiltless by Christ (Matt. 12:3f.). In each case there was not only no divine condemnation for the moral law they "broke" (or better, did not follow) but, contrariwise, there was evident divine approval. The same is true of other, similar cases in which moral commands to obey parents (Luke 2:41f.) or God-ordained authorities are concerned (e.g. Exod. 12; Acts 4–5; Rev. 13).

---

9. Plato gives a similar illustration in the *Republic* (Part I, Book I). He says, "Suppose, for example, a friend who had lent us a weapon were to go mad and then ask for it back; surely anyone would say we ought not to return it. It would not be 'right' to do so."

Graded Absolutism Is True

Therefore, in real (unavoidable) moral conflicts, God does not hold a person guilty for not keeping a lower moral law so long as he keeps the higher. That is, God exempts one from his duty to keep the lower law since he could not keep it without breaking a higher law. This exemption functions something like an ethical "right of way" law. In many states the law declares that when two cars simultaneously reach an intersection without signals or signs, the car on the right has the right of way. Common sense dictates that they both cannot go through the intersection at the same time; one car must yield. Similarly, when a person enters an ethical "intersection" where two laws come into unavoidable conflict, it is evident that one law must "yield" to the other.

An Elaboration of Graded Absolutism

The most obvious and basic of all divisions or levels of duty is between the command to love God and the command to love one's neighbor.

Love for God over Love for Man

Jesus explicitly declares one commandment to be the "first" and "greatest." Further, He teaches (Matt. 22:36-38) that one's love for God should be so much more than his love for parents that the love for the latter would look like "hate" by contrast (Luke 14:26). One implication of this is that if parents teach a child to hate God, the child must disobey the parents in order to obey God. This is true despite the fact that the Bible enjoins children to "be obedient to parents in all things" (Col. 3:20). The fact that the parallel passage in Ephesians (6:1) adds, "in the Lord" indicates that a hierarchy is envisioned which places the filial duty on a lower level, under the duty to love and obey God.

Obey God over Government

God ordained human government (Gen. 9:6) and commands the Christian to "submit" to those in authority even if they are evil men (Rom. 13:1f.; Titus 3:1). Peter goes so far as to say we should submit ourselves "to every ordinance of man for the Lord's sake" (I Peter 2:13).

The attempt of some to differentiate between submission and obedience—and thus claim that Christians need only submit but not obey government—fails for several reasons. First, it is plainly opposed to the spirit of the passages which enjoin Christians to follow the laws of their land. Second, the passage in First Peter demands submission to "every ordinance," not merely to the consequences of disobeying an ordinance. And submission to a law is obedience. Third, the word *submission* as used in the New Testament implies obedience. It was, for example, what a slave was to do to his master (Col. 3:22). Finally, the words *submission* and *obedience* are used in parallel in the Titus passage (3:1); thus Christians are told "to obey" governmental authorities.

It is clear that Christians are commanded of God to obey government. Hence, when disobedience to government is approved of God, it is clearly in view of a higher moral law. Several biblical instances illustrate this point. First, worship of God is higher than any command of government (Dan. 3). Second, no governmental law against private prayer should be obeyed (Dan. 6). Further, if a government commands a believer not to preach the gospel (Acts 4, 5),[10] or if it decrees participation in idolatry (Dan. 3) or even the murder of innocent victims (Exod. 1), it should not be obeyed. In each case the moral

---

10. In this case the "authorities" were religious but not civil. Even so, Jesus enjoined obedience to Judaism's religious authorities (Matt. 23:2).

obligation to pray, worship God, preach the gospel, and so forth, is higher.

Life-Saving (Mercy) over Truth-Telling

There is no question that the Bible commands Christians not "to bear false witness" (Exod. 20:16). We are also told, "let every one speak the truth with his neighbor," (Eph. 4:25). Indeed, deception and lying are repeatedly condemned in Scripture (See Prov. 12:22; 19:5; Rev. 21:8).

On the other hand, the Bible indicates that there are occasions when lying is justifiable. Rahab lied to save the lives of Israel's spies and was immortalized in the Book of Hebrews "Hall of Fame" (Heb. 11). It should be noted that first, nowhere does the Bible condemn her for this lie; second, her lie was an integral part of the act of mercy she showed in saving the spies' lives; and third, the Bible says, "Rahab . . . shall live, because she hid the messengers that we sent" (Josh. 6:17). But the real concealment was accomplished by the deception of Rahab. Hence, her "lie"[11] was an integral part of her faith for which she was commended of God (Heb. 11:31; James 2:25).

In the story of the Hebrew midwives we have an even clearer case of divinely approved lying to save a life. For the Scriptures say, "God dealt well with the midwives; and. . . . he gave them families." (Exod. 1:20, 21). Nowhere in the text does God ever say they were blessed only for their mercy and in spite of their lie. Indeed, the lie was part of the mercy shown.

---

11. Some would prefer calling this not a "lie" but an "intentional falsification." Call it what we will, it does not change the fact that it would be morally wrong—unless, of course, one is obeying a higher moral law in so doing. I prefer calling it a "lie" so that it is clearly understood that lying as such (without a higher conflicting law) is wrong.

It should not be surprising that mercy is considered to be higher than truth. Common sense dictates that Corrie Ten Boom's acts of mercy to the Jews, which involved lying to the Nazis, were not evil but good. Indeed, those who say that one should not lie to save a life are inconsistent, for they lie to save their property: they leave their lights on when they are away from home in order to intentionally deceive potential theives.

There are other biblical examples of graded absolutism, but these will suffice to illustrate that there are "weightier matters" of the law and greater and lesser commands of God. It is the Christian's obligation in every morally conflicting situation to search the Scriptures for an answer. If one does not know what to do in certain situations, he should heed Jesus' words, "You are mistaken, because you know neither the scriptures nor the power of God . . ." (Matt. 22:29, NEB).

A Defense of Graded Absolutism

A number of objections have been raised against this kind of hierarchical or graded absolutism since it was presented some years ago.[12] The following is a list of objections and responses that have come to my attention.

1. *How does graded absolutism differ from Joseph Fletcher's situationism?*[13]

First, Fletcher does not believe there are any contentful

---

12. I first proposed this view in 1971 in *Ethics: Alternatives and Issues* (Grand Rapids: Zondervan).

13. Despite the fact that I have taken large sections of two books as well as two major articles to denounce "situation ethics," strangely enough some have included my view in books dedicated to attacking situation ethics (see Erwin Lutzer, *Morality Gap*). Another has suggested my view may be "ethical latitudinarianism" (Walter Kaiser, "The Weightier and Lighter Matters of the Law," p. 185, n. 32).

absolutes; graded absolutism does. According to graded absolutism, the universal commands of Scripture, for example, such as the prohibitions against blasphemy, idolatry, adultery, murder, lying, and so forth, are absolutely binding on all men at all times and all places. Second, graded absolutism holds that there are more absolutes than one, as indicated above. Fletcher believes in one and only one absolute, and that absolute is formal and empty. Third, Fletcher believes that the situation *determines* what one should do in a given case; graded absolutism holds that situational factors only help one to *discover* what God has determined that we should do. That is, the situation does not fill an empty absolute with content and thereby determine what one should do. Rather, the situational factors merely help one discover which command of God is applicable to that particular case.

2. *Despite the differences in theory, do not graded absolutism and situationism come to many of the same conclusions concerning what one ought to do?*

This question wrongly assumes that there is only a theoretical difference between the views. It is true that occasionally the conclusions are the same, but they are based on very different reasons. Hence, the similarities are only accidental and not essential. Fletcher concludes something is right or wrong because the "existential particularities" of the situation determine it; graded absolutism, on the other hand, concludes something is right or wrong because God has declared it. Furthermore, there are numerous and significant differences in conclusion between situationism and graded absolutism. For example, in contrast to Fletcher, I do not hold that wife-swapping is ever right, that one should commit adultery to get out of prison, that one should ever blaspheme, that abortion of unwanted babies is justified, that harlotry to teach maturity is right, that premarital intercourse is justifiable, and so on. In brief, whether in principle or practice, any relation to situationism is purely coincidental. Indeed, the same accidental similarities could be drawn between most other views and situationism.

3. *Does not graded absolutism open the door to subjectivism,
   with each one deciding for himself what is the greatest
   good?*

There is nothing to hinder someone proposing this kind of
subjective hierarchicalism, where every individual decides
for himself what is best. However, this is emphatically *not*
what we have proposed. The Christian does not decide for
himself what are the ethical priorities. It is God who
established the pyramid of values in accordance with His
own nature. These are recorded in Scripture and, hence,
they are no more subjective than is any other ethic subject to
biblical exegesis. The hierarchy is objective and determined
by God; the only subjective factors are our understanding
and acceptance of God's values. So far as I can tell this is a
limitation shared by every other Christian view as well.

4. *If there can be real conflicts among absolute norms, then in
   what sense can they be called absolute?*

As I stated in the *Christian Ethic of Love* (Zondervan,
1973), there are three ways in which hierarchicalism is an
absolutism. First, all norms are based in the absoluteness of
God. God does not change, and principles based on His
nature are likewise unchanging. Second, each particular
command is absolute *as such*. It is only when there is a conflict of relationship that appeal must be made to the higher
in order to resolve the conflict. Third, the very gradation of
values by which the conflicts are resolved is absolute. For
example, it is absolutely established in accordance with the
nature of God that in an unavoidable conflict between God
and parent one must put God first. In brief, hierarchicalism
is an absolutism in three ways: by virtue of its basis in God,
in the context of each command, and in the very nature of
the hierarchy that resolves the conflicts.

5. *If God is one in essence and if His nature is the basis for all
   absolute moral principles, how then can there be more
   than one absolute moral norm?*

God is one in essence, but He has many attributes. Each of
these is absolute insofar as it reflects His nature. Likewise,

the moral laws based on the unchanging characteristics of God are many but each are, nevertheless, absolute. God is the one absolute basis for all laws that reflect His nature, and each law is absolutely binding on the particular activity it governs.

6. *Is there a hierarchy within God that serves as a basis for the gradation within the moral laws?*

There need be no hierarchy within God's essence. Indeed, if God is absolutely one in essence and if it takes many elements to form a hierarchy, then there can be no hierarchy in God's essence. It is *possible*, however, that there is a hierarchy in God's attributes, with, for example, love taking priority over holiness. But even this view is not necessary to graded absolutism.

It could be that the hierarchy is only within the exercise of God's will in the world in accordance with His attributes, that it is a hierarchy of application of God's attributes. All the many moral attributes may be one in God, but these could be diffused into many laws, ranging from higher to lower as they pass through the prism of the finite world. In any case, it is sufficient for graded absolutism that the hierarchy is revealed by God and that it reflects the absolute nature of God.

7. *Did Jesus ever face any real moral conflicts?*

The Bible teaches that Jesus was tempted in all points as we are and that He is our complete moral example. Certainly there would be something lacking in the basis for a Christian ethic if the paradigm of our morality did not face the most difficult kinds of situations that we His followers face.

Some specific examples of moral conflicts in Jesus' life are: obedience to parents or to God (when He was twelve); obeying the Sabbath regulations or doing good; obedience to government or to God. The greatest conflict Christ faced is often overlooked, specifically, the trial and crucifixion. He was squeezed between the demands of justice for the innocent (Himself) and love for the guilty (mankind). It is noteworthy that He chose love for the many over justice for the one. This conflict was without question the greatest ever faced by man, and it dramatizes the supremacy of love over justice in unavoidable conflicts.

8. *Do we ever create our own moral conflicts and should we therefore be held guilty rather than being exempt from doing the supposed "greater good"?*

We do sometimes create our own conflicts, and in those cases we are guilty. If we make our moral "bed" then we must lie in it. However, it is a mistake to suppose that all moral conflicts stem from previous personal sins. Sometimes it is one's virtues that help precipitate a moral conflict. Note the story of Daniel and the three Hebrew children (Dan. 3). At other times it is neither one's sin nor his righteousness that occasions a real conflict. Two examples are the question of abortion to save a mother's life, and whether an innocent person held at gunpoint should divulge information that would lead to the death of an innocent person. It is to these kinds of personally unavoidable conflicts that graded absolutism is addressed. And both Scripture and human experience provide significant and numerous examples of these real but unavoidable conflicts.

9. *How can a lesser evil ever be the good thing to do? Is this nothing more than pronouncing evil good?*

An evil as such is never good. The hierarchical view does not proclaim that the evil is a good thing to do, but asserts that the highest obligation in the conflict is the *good* thing to do. For example, in lying to save a life it is not the lie that is good (a lie *as such* is always wrong), but it is the intent and action to save a life that is good—despite the fact that intentional falsification was necessary to accomplish this good. In other words, it is unfortunately true that what is called "evil" sometimes accompanies the performance of good acts. In these cases God does not consider a man culpable for the concomitant "evil" in view of the performance of the greater good.

In this respect, graded absolutism is similar to the principle of double effect, which notes that when two results—a good result and an evil result—emerge from one act, the individual is held responsible only for the good one he intended and not the evil one which necessarily resulted from the good intention. For example, when a doctor amputates to save a life, he is not morally culpable for maiming but is to be morally praised for life-saving.

10. *In the final analysis, is not graded absolutism a utilitarianism, since it resolves conflicts by asking which alternative brings the greatest good?*

Actually, just the reverse is true. Utilitarianism reduces to deontological (duty) ethics in the final analysis, because it needs some intrinsic values and norms by which it can judge what will bring the greatest good in the long run. The differences between a deontological ethic such as hierarchicalism and a teleological ethic such as utilitarianism were pointed out in great detail in chapter one of *Ethics: Alternatives and Issues* (Zondervan, 1971), and in chapter three were noted specific criticisms of a utilitarian ethic.

Hierarchicalism does not resolve ethical conflicts by an appeal to an extrinsic end (what will bring the greatest good to the greatest number), but to a higher intrinsic norm as revealed by God. Of course, any ethic is obliged to look at the results of actions, but this does not make them utilitarian. For example, we would not call a parent utilitarian for pulling his child away from the edge of the cliff, nor would we consider a doctor to be ethically teleological if he gave antibiotics to a patient. Even the most rigid legalistic ethic must operate on the calculation of at-hand results. This is a far cry, however, from basing one's whole ethic on the projected estimation of the long-range results for the most of mankind. Graded absolutism, in contrast to utilitarianism, holds that following right rules (specifically, God's) will bring about the best results. It does not believe that man's calculation of the best results will determine what the best rules should be. We keep the rules and leave the long-run consequences to God.

11. *Is not the alleged distinction between an exemption and an*

exception, used to support graded absolutism, merely a
semantical and not a real difference?

The difference is more than verbal. First of all, an exception would violate the universality and absoluteness of a norm, whereas an exemption does not. That is, if there is an exception, then the law is not absolute and hence does not reflect the nature of God, but at best describes only what is *generally* the right course of action. Absolute norms, on the contrary, are based on God's unchanging nature and have no exceptions. If they did, it would be much like saying that God is at times untruthful or hateful. Second, an exception means that the act as such is actually a good act in that given circumstance. Not so with an exemption. The act as such (say, lying) is always wrong; it is the life-saving activity, of which the lie is a necessary concomitant, that is good—not the lie as such. Third, in an exception, the general rule is not binding on that particular case, and so there is no real conflict. However, where an exemption is made following a universal law, the law is still binding and the conflict is real. For instance, the law of filial piety is still binding on the child when he refuses to obey his parents' command to worship an idol; that is precisely what makes the conflict real. Finally, an exemption only eliminates the individual's culpability in not performing the demands of a law; it in no way changes either the basis or the nature of the law as absolute. An exception, on the other hand, would prove the law not to be absolute.

The difference between an exemption and an exception can be illustrated as follows. When one kills another human being in self-defense, he is exempt from guilt. Yet there is no exception made to the law which requires us to always treat another man—even a would-be murderer—as a human (that is, with intrinsic value). There was never a moment when the potential murderer ceased to be human. If there were, then there would be a legitimate exception to the law of human treatment. However, despite the fact that he was always human and that the law to treat him as such still stands, the potential victim is exempt from the moral consequences of disobeying this law in view of the overriding value of defending his own innocent life.

12. *How can the graded absolutist hold that there are real moral conflicts when he claims there is a resolution for them in keeping the higher law?*

This question wrongly assumes that whatever was resolved was not a real and inevitable conflict. If this were so then any conflict that is ultimately resolved would turn out to be only apparent or illusory. Surely no biblical theist would seriously hold that the conflict between good and evil is not real simply because it will be resolved in the *eschaton* (end). Nor does the fact that one triumphs over temptation make the sin-allurement unreal.

Unless one by simple stipulative definition decrees that whatever resolved is not a real conflict, then this question seems pointless. Moral conflict can be real and unavoidable and yet yield to final resolution, with the lower yielding to the higher. We say that the conflict was "irresolvable" only in the sense that there was no "give" in the force of the commands. Neither law "backed down"; both continued to demand with the same absoluteness that is theirs by virtue of their grounding in God. That is, God's absolute nature does not change simply because finite and fallible man finds himself in unavoidable moral conflicts. God intervenes in love and exempts a man from the demands of a command which cannot be kept without breaking a higher command. Technically speaking, however, the conflict is not "irresolvable" but only unavoidable, since the conflict is resolved by obeying the higher law.

13. *How can a moral principle be absolutely binding if it can sometimes be broken without guilt?*

Actually, the lower command is not really "broken" when the higher command is followed. We do not say that a magnet "breaks" the law of gravity in attracting a nail, nor that killing in self-defense "violates" the law of respect and preservation of human beings. The overriding duty to keep the higher law simply renders it unnecessary for us to perform the demands of the lesser command.

The command remains absolute even when it is not followed, for its absoluteness is based in the nature of God and not in its performance by man. The nature of truth does not change when men tell justifiable falsehoods in order to save innocent lives. If the real conflict is between truth-telling and mercy-showing, both of which are grounded in God's nature, then there is no conflict between these in the nature of God. God is one, and all His attributes are harmonious. The real conflict is that on some occasions a man cannot perform both. In these cases God withholds culpability from the man who shows mercy to the innocent rather than telling truth to the guilty. But this in no way means that both commands are not binding at all times; God never ceases to manifest absolutely what is absolutely right. However, in unavoidable clashes, God does not demand obedience to lower laws, nor does He exact personal culpability.

14. *How can lying ever flow from the nature of God as true?*

It doesn't; it flows from the nature of God *as merciful.* God is both merciful and true. Graded absolutism holds that when truth and mercy conflict, then the necessary act of mercy (in this case, lying) finds its basis in God's nature as merciful. Hence justifiable lies are not based in God's truthfulness but in His mercy.

15. *Does not graded absolutism deny the doctrine of total depravity by assuming all sins are avoidable?*

Total depravity does not mean that all sin is unavoidable. This would contradict I Corinthians 10:13, which states that all sin is avoidable. Depravity means it is inevitable that fallen men will sin, but not that sin is unavoidable. Sin is unavoidable by fallen man on his own, but all sin is avoidable by God's grace.[14]

---

14. The substance of this section was first published in *The Trinity Journal* in an article titled, "In Defense of Hierarchical Ethics," vol. 4 (Spring, 1975): 82-87.

Conclusion

We have surveyed the three options available to evangelical ethics—unqualified absolutism, conflicting absolutism, and graded absolutism. The first two have been found wanting. Graded absolutism seems to be the only viable option. It both preserves moral absolutes and yet provides a realistic approach to genuine moral conflicts.

Chapter **6**

Options and Implications

Each evangelical option in ethics is based on certain presuppositions and carries with it certain implications. Since we have already discussed the central premises of each view, we will now turn our attention to the implications.

Implications for Theology

There are certain implications for theology entailed in the various ethical views. It would probably be more proper to say that different theological positions have implications for different ethical views. It may be of interest to note first of all that, consistently or not, the Anabaptist tradition has tended to hold unqualified absolutism, the Lutheran tradition has fit better with conflicting absolutism, and the Reformed tradition is more compatible with graded absolutism. An analysis of the reasons for these alliances is outside the scope of this discussion; we will proceed to speak here only of some logical connections between theology and ethics.

Implications for the Doctrine of God

Since we have defended graded absolutism, we will now relate the theological implications to that position. The implications for the other positions will be drawn as well.

God's nature and will. Graded absolutism implies that God is absolute and unchanging, and that His will does not operate in isolation from His moral nature. In short, it implies an ethical essentialism and not a pure voluntarism in God. In other words, God is not arbitrary about what is right or wrong. Something is right not simply because God wills it, but He wills it because it is right (in accordance with His unchanging character). Graded absolutism also implies that God has many moral attributes (truth, goodness, justice, and so on); each one is the basis of a different moral absolute. Further, graded absolutism implies that God anticipated the fall of man and the resulting moral conflicts and designed a way out for any morally responsible being. Finally, God's fairness in dealing with all men is implied in that He does not blame anyone for the unavoidable. In addition, graded absolutism implies that God's moral attributes are hierarchically arranged, if not in Himself, then at least as they are revealed in the moral laws.[1] God's mercy, for example, takes precedence over His justice, so long as His justice is satisfied (cf. the cross).

By contrast, the other views assume either that all moral attributes (laws) are of equal weight, or (as in Hodge) that truth is higher than life-saving, since the

---

1. The revealed hierarchy of the moral law may be likened to light passing through a prism. The light ray is one in itself but becomes a whole spectrum of colors when it shines through a prism. In like manner, all moral laws have an absolute unity in God but become many as they are revealed through the "prism" of the finite world.

latter flows only from God's will but not His nature. The problem with this is that life-saving is an act of mercy and, therefore, by logical implication, this would mean truth is of higher moral value to God than mercy.

Man's nature and will. Augustine's form of absolutism entails a dualistic view of man wherein the soul is higher than the body.[2] This is not so for graded absolutism. Rather graded absolutism implies the unity of man, who comes as a whole under each command of God, and the unity of the moral law, which never stands in unresolved tension. By contrast, conflicting absolutism assumes that God's law has unity only in God's nature and will, but not as it applies in this world.

The kingdom of God and future things. Conflicting absolutism would seem to imply an amillennial view in which the kingdom of God can never really be fully achieved in this world. A premillennial view, on the other hand, fits well with graded absolutism, since unity and moral perfection can be achieved in the world which contains moral conflicts such as a real finite world has.

Christ and the cross. Perhaps the most sobering implication of all is that fact that only in the view of graded absolutism does the substitutionary atonement make sense. Indeed, in the lesser-evil view of moral conflicts the cross would be an evil, albeit, the lesser evil. And in unqualified or non-conflicting absolutism, incredibly, the moral conflict of the cross is not *real!*

The Christian and society [ethics and politics]. In non-conflicting absolutism, political participation in a pagan society is ruled out, since living and acting in a real (and

---

2. See discussion in chapter 3.

sinful) world is always less than God's ideal. And anything less than God's ideal or perfect standard is sinful. Or, in the lesser-evil view, regular (even daily) actions in conflict situations—which doctors, lawyers, and legislators face all the time—would be evil and would demand constant confession of guilt. However, in graded absolutism, full, guiltless participation in the social and political process is possible.

Further, the graded absolutist does not need to legislate Christian morality on a non-Christian society. He need not work for laws to achieve the maximal Christian ethic (only a millennium could bring that about), nor need he settle for a society of little or no morals. Rather, the Christian legislator should: (1) personally exemplify the maximal Christian ethic; (2) personally and ecclesiastically work to convert everyone possible so that they, too, will work toward exemplifying the maximal Christian ethic; and yet (3) legally and socially vote for those laws that will permit non-Christians the freedom not to live by Christian standards (nor should non-Christians force Christians to live by pagan standards).

The Christian attitude toward strong alcoholic beverages is a case in point. Let us say that abstinence from strong and excessive drink of an alcoholic beverage is the maximal Christian ethic (Prov. 20:1; I Tim. 3:3). If this is so, the Christian should personally live this way, preach and teach this is right, and try to convert all alcoholics and convince them to adopt this policy. However, the Christian should *not* vote for total prohibition so that no non-Christian can have strong drink. This would be a violation of the free choice of the non-Christian. However, the Christian can legitimately vote for certain laws against drunk driving, since the Christian's life is being endangered by drunk drivers. The main point, however, is this: the Christian's personal standards of ethics and the laws he would socially and legally support for non-Christians may be different.

These suggested theological implications of the options in Christian ethics barely scratch the surface of some of the more apparent implications of the views. A complete analysis would require another book. These, however, are sufficient enough to focus attention on the systemic significance for theology of accepting one ethical option over another. In short, an ethical system cannot be chosen in isolation from a theological system. Indeed, it cannot be chosen without implying a theological position of some kind.

Implications for Psychology

Guilt is a major problem for the human psyche. A student who once held the conflicting absolutism view shared with me his tremendous sense of relief upon discovering that sin was not unavoidable. The graded absolutism he came to accept had relieved him of the plaguing necessity of unavoidable guilt and constant and unnecessary confession. When he discovered that God did not blame him for doing his best in conflict situations, his self-image and worth increased measurably. Graded absolutism, then, is an important answer to one of the human psyche's most agonizing problems, the problem of psychological guilt. This is not to deny that often our guilt is justifiable moral guilt. It is simply to point out that some guilt is merely psychological (not moral) and thus avoidable.

Implications for Society and Politics

Evangelicals have often been accused of non-participation in the social and political affairs of the

world, of being so heavenly minded that they are no
earthly good.[3] This charge is understandably applicable
to a non-conflicting absolutist, especially of the Augustinian variety. For according to that view, the spiritual is of
higher value than the material. Hence, it follows logically
that one's preoccupation would be with the "higher"
spiritual world. Further, since one's unqualified and absolute duty is to God and not to a human authority or
sphere, any social action taken that is less than God's
ideal and perfect standard is sin. And how many actions
in this real (sinful) world are ideal? Hence, in the unqualified absolutism view, a Christian would be con-
tinually and knowingly sinning by his very participation in
the social and political arenas.[4] Complete isolation from
the world is the logical conclusion of this view, for there is
no way a Christian should be personally involved in
politics. Christian congressmen would by the nature of
their profession (as well as would business men, doctors,
lawyers, policemen, and anyone facing moral conflicts in
their profession) be constantly and unavoidably sinning.

On the other hand, the graded absolutist can conscien-
tiously participate in the less than ideal social order,
knowing that his guiltless duty is only to follow the highest
moral law in every real conflict.

Implications for Ethics

There are two important implications for Christian
ethics which graded absolutism offers. Both have to do
with avoiding the extremes of relativism and legalism.

3. David Moberg's challenge in this regard is noteworthy. See his
Inasmuch (Grand Rapids: Eerdmans, 1965).
4. As we noted in another connection (war) in *Ethics: Alternatives
and Issues* (Grand Rapids: Zondervan, 1971), chapter 9, unqualified absolutism, when carried through consistently, leads to political and
social "dropout-ism."

The first implication for Christian ethics is that mere human actions as such are not intrinsically good or evil. Even the unqualified absolutists admit that some actions (such as giving to the poor) are neither good nor bad as such, but depend on the purpose for which they are performed. But unqualified absolutists fail to appreciate the fact that this is true of other actions as well, such as intentional falsification (lying). It would also apply to the mutilation of a human body, an action which, like lying, is wrong when done with unworthy motives. But when the purpose of amputation is to save a life, then the action of mutilation becomes good. Graded absolutism releases given human actions from the legalistic clutches of a necessary association with evil. Simply because a given action is usually associated with evil does not mean that the same action performed for a different purpose (that is, in obedience to a higher moral law) cannot sometimes be morally good. In making this distinction, one is following both the example of Jesus and that of the apostle Paul. Even though the Sabbath command was one of the Ten Commandments, Jesus made it clear that a rigid identification of certain actions (which would normally violate the Sabbath) with evil was a suffocating legalism. In response, Jesus pointed out that there was a higher law than the Sabbath, namely, the law of mercy. "The sabbath was made for man, not man for the sabbath" (Mark 2:27). Likewise, the apostle Paul made it clear that some of the highest and seemingly most altruistic of human actions (giving all to the poor and sacrificing one's life for others) can be loveless and not morally praiseworthy (I Cor. 13:3). And actions always associated with evil (for example, rape, killing one's children) are evil because the motive was always evil, not because the act as such was evil. If actions were evil apart from human intentions, then animals or imbeciles who performed the same actions would also be morally culpable. It is not an action as such which is evil but an intention-action complex. That is, it is an intended action in view of a moral law which has moral significance and not simply the action itself. Just as the same word in a different context can have a different meaning, the same action in a different moral context can have a different moral significance.

A second ethical implication of graded absolutism is the important distinction between the function of the situation or circumstances and ethical norms. In situation ethics (such as Joseph Fletcher's), the circumstances determine what is right and what is wrong.[5] For the graded absolutist, however, the situation does not determine what is right; it merely helps us discover which absolute moral principle applies. Or, stated another way, the circumstances do not determine what is right; they simply help one to discover which moral law applies in that situation. In actuality, nearly everyone operates this way in daily life. There are often two or more obligations binding at one time. In order to discover which one should be followed, we take a look at all the facts so that we can discover which moral duty we ought to obey.

C. S. Lewis's illustration about witches is instructive in this regard.[6] In early America witches were burned, but today they are not. This is not, says Lewis, because our values have changed. Rather, it is because our factual understanding of what witches can do has changed. In early America the factual understanding was that witches could murder people by their curses, spells, and so forth. Today, the factual understanding is that witches

---

5. See Fletcher, *Situation Ethics: The New Morality* (Philadelphia: Westminster Press, 1966), chapter 8.

6. See C. S. Lewis, *Mere Christianity* (New York: Macmillan, 1964).

do not have these powers. The moral principle, however, remains the same, namely, "murderers should be punished as murders." The same point can be illustrated from the Vietnam War. Those who understood the facts to be that America was defending an innocent, autonomous government against evil outside aggressors naturally believed the war to be justified. On the other hand, those who saw the American presence in southeast Asia as a foreign and unnecessary interference in a civil war on the side of an evil government, a war without popular support and with no U.S. constitutional basis for involvement, understandably believed the war to be wrong. The basic difference was not one of value; rather, it was one of factual understanding.

Hence, even the same event can sometimes call for different courses of action by different Christians, depending on their factual understanding of the circumstances. One must remember what Paul said in this context, namely, "Let every man be fully persuaded in his own mind" (Rom. 14:5). Christians should be very careful in calling the actions of another person evil simply because those actions are often (even usually) associated with evil. We cannot always be sure of the motives the other person had in performing the action. Jesus told us not to judge the motives of another (Matt. 7:1), for God is the seer and revealer of human hearts (Luke 12:2; Heb. 4:13; I Cor. 3:11f.).

Implications for Biblical Inspiration

Strange as it may seem, there is one very important implication of graded absolutism for the subject of biblical inspiration. It has been argued by some modern thinkers that human language is so tainted with sin that it is incapable of any purely sinless expressions of truth.[7] (Some have applied the same thinking to Jesus' humanity, insisting that it, too, partakes of human iniquity as well as human frailty.)

Their position can be outlined as follows:

(1) Total depravity makes sin unavoidable.
(2) Human language is an expression of totally depraved beings.
(3) The Bible is written in human language.
(4) Therefore, sin is unavoidably expressed in the very language of the Bible.

The alternatives to this conclusion are all undesirable for the evangelical. First, one could admit with the neo-orthodox (contrary to the teaching of Christ and Scripture)[8] that the words of Scripture are not the Word of God, but simply an erring (even sinful) human record of God's revelation to the prophets. Second, one could argue (unscripturally and inconsistently) that an absolutely perfect God can speak morally imperfect words. Since neither of these alternatives is open to an evangelical, he must reject one of more of the premises of the above argument. An evangelical would not want to deny either premise (2) or (3), since the Bible was indeed written by human beings in human language and since these human beings were totally depraved. This leaves only premise (1) to discard. But the conflicting absolutist holds this premise to be true. Indeed, it is at the very heart of his view that at least some sin is unavoidable.

---

7. Some neo-orthodox thinkers hold this view, and even Berkouwer comes dangerously close to this. See his *Studies in Dogmatics: Holy Scripture* (Grand Rapids: Eerdmans, 1975), pp. 205, 206.

8. See chapter 2.

On the other hand, the unqualified absolutist does not seem to appreciate the fact that premise (2) is contrary to his view. For according to nonconflicting or unqualified absolutism, there is never a real unavoidable conflict wherein one cannot obey a moral law. But if human language is an expression of depraved beings, then how can sin be avoided in using it? What makes the dilemma particularly acute for the unqualified absolutist is that he identifies given actions and words as such with evil, apart from the motive or purpose of the one performing them. If this were the case, then any expression in Scripture that is used in an evil way by men would also be evil when used by God in Scripture. Further, on this basis the very terms *God, Christ,* and *hell* would be evil when used in Scripture, since these are regularly used by unbelievers in a profane way.

The obvious answer to this problem is not open to the unqualified absolutist, namely, that usage determines meaning. For if the word (or act) changes its moral value (from evil to good) when used for a good purpose or in a good context, then this is exactly what graded absolutism argues. The apparent conclusion of this analysis is that only in the graded absolutism ethical view does one have an adequate answer to the neo-orthodox charge that biblical language is necessarily tainted with sin and, therefore, not verbally inspired.[9]

Conclusion

Which ethical option an evangelical adopts has significant implications in numerous areas. This should be no surprise to anyone who believes in the unity of truth.

---

9. For a further defense of biblical inspiration against contemporary charges see Norman L. Geisler, ed., *Inerrancy* (Grand Rapids: Zondervan, 1980).

There may, however, be surprises for evangelicals who begin to work out these implications consistently. It seems clear that many evangelicals will either have to give up certain theological positions they espouse or else change their ethical view. My own hope is that evangelicals will increasingly see the value of graded absolutism. It is not only consistent with biblical Christianity, but also provides a viable answer to many problems in both Scripture and society.

Bibliography

Abbot, Francis. *Kant's Critique of Practical Reason.* London: Longmans, Green and Co., Ltd., 1909.

Abelard, Peter. *Abelard's Ethics.* Vol. 3. Translated by J. R. McCallum. Oxford: Blackwell, 1935.

Allen, Reginald E., ed. *Greek Philosophy: Thales to Aristotle.* New York: Macmillan, 1966.

Aquinas, St. Thomas. *Summa Theologica.* Book I.

Augustine. *Against Lying.*

_____. *City of God.*

_____. *On Lying.*

Ayer, A. J. *Language, Truth and Logic,* 2d ed. New York: Dover Publications, 1936.

Bentham, Jeremy. *Introduction to Principles of Morals and Legislation.* Oxford, 1789.

Berkouwer, Gerrit C. *Studies in Dogmatics: Holy Scripture.* Grand Rapids: Eerdmans, 1975.

Biel, Gabriel. *Collectorium.*

Carnell, Edward J. *Christian Commitment.* Grand Rapids: Eerdmans, 1957.

Erickson, Millard J. *Relativism in Contemporary Ethics.* Grand Rapids: Baker Book House, 1974.

Fletcher, Joseph. *Situation Ethics: The New Morality.* Philadelphia: Westminster Press, 1966.

Geisler, Norman L. *The Christian Ethic of Love.* Grand Rapids: Zondervan, 1973.

_____. *Ethics: Alternatives and Issues.* Grand Rapids: Zondervan, 1971.

Geisler, Norman L., ed. *Inerrancy.* Grand Rapids: Zondervan, 1980.

Geisler, Norman L., and Feinberg, Paul D. *Introduction to Philosophy.* Grand Rapids: Baker Book House, 1980.

Gilson, E. *History of Christian Philosophy.* Westminster, Md.; Christian Classics, reprint.

Hawthorne, Gerald F. *Current Issues in Biblical and Patristic Interpretation.* Grand Rapids: Eerdmans, 1975.

Henry, Carl. *Aspects of Christian Social Ethics.* Grand Rapids: Eerdmans, 1964.

_____. *Christian Personal Ethics.* Grand Rapids: Eerdmans, 1957.

Hirsh, E. D. *Validity in Interpretation.* New Haven: Yale University Press, 1967.

Huxley, Julian. *Collected Essays.* London, 1893-94.

Kierkegaard, Sören. *Fear and Trembling.* New York: Doubleday, 1954.

Ladd, George. *The Pattern of New Testament Truth.* Grand Rapids, Eerdmans, 1968.

Lewis, C. S. *Mere Christianity.* New York: Macmillan, 1964.

_____. *The Abolition of Man.* New York: Macmillan, 1962.

Lutzer, Erwin. *The Morality Gap.* Chicago: Moody Press, 1972.

McCormick, R., and Ramsey, P., eds. *Doing Evil to Achieve Good: Moral Choice in Conflict Situations.* Chicago: Loyola University Press, 1978.

Moberg, David. *Inasmuch.* Grand Rapids: Eerdmans, 1965.

Montgomery, John W. *Situation Ethics.* Minneapolis: Bethany Fellowship, 1972.

Morrison, Frank. *Who Moved the Stone?* Downers Grove, Ill.: InterVarsity, 1958.

Murray, John. *Principles of Conduct.* Grand Rapids: Eerdmans, 1957.

Nietzsche, Friedrich. *Beyond Good and Evil.* Chicago: Henry Regnery, 1966.

Owen, H. P. *The Moral Argument for Christian Theism.* New York: Humanities Press, 1965.

Plato. *Republic.* Book I.

Russell, Bertrand. *The Basic Writing of Bertrand Russell.* Edited by Robert E. Egner and Lester E. Dennon. New York: Simon and Schuster, 1961.

_____. *Human Society in Ethics and Politics.* New York: Mentor, 1962.

Sartre, Jean-Paul. *Being and Nothingness.* New York: Washington Square Press, 1966.

_____. *No Exit and Three Other Plays.* New York: Collier-Macmillan, 1966.

Saunders, Jason, ed. *Greek and Roman Philosophy After Aristotle.* New York: Macmillan, 1966.

Tillich, Paul, *Ultimate Concern.* London: SCM Press, 1965.

Trueblood, David Elton. *Philosophy of Religion.* New York: Harper, 1957.

William of Ockham. *Commentary on the Sentences.* Vol. 2.

_____. *De Principiis Theologiae.*

Index

Abelard, Peter, 12
absolutes, 22, 23, 24, 35, 37, 54, 93, 98
absolutism, 9, 20, 23, 35, 36; unqualified, 43-65, 76, 101, 103, 108 (also n.4), 109, 113; graded, 61, 62, 81-101, 103, 105, 106, 107, 108, 110, 111, 113, 114, see also hierarchicalism; conflicting, 67-80, 101, 103, 105, 112; ideal, 67 n.2; non-conflicting, 67 n.2, 105, 108, 113
Anabaptist tradition, 103
antinomianism, 18, 20, 21-23
Aquinas, Thomas, 27 n.2
atheism, 19
Augustine, St., 43, 44-49, 50, 51, 52, 54-56, 58, 59, 60, 105, 108
Ayer, A. J., 18, 21, 34 n.5, 35

Barth, Karl, 30
Bentham, Jeremy, 15
Berkouwer, G. C., 112 n.7
Bible (special revelation), 22-23, 24, 27, 30, 31-36, 39-40, 112

body-soul dualism, 46, 54-55, 105, 108

Carnell, E. J., 67 n.1
categorical imperative, 49, 51
certainty, 45, 56
Christ, 9, 28, 38-39, 41, 70, 75-80, 86; incarnation of, 32, 36, 39; as moral example, 39, 79, 80, 95
Christian ethic, 25, 27, 36, 37, 39 41, 65, 71; implications of, 105-114
conflicts (dilemmas), moral, 43, 52, 53, 56-58, 61, 62, 63, 64, 65, 67-80, 99, 101, 105, 106
Cratylus, 10

Darwin, Charles, 17
Domiurgo, 27
deontological ethics, 97
Dewey, John, 22-23
double effect, principle of, 96
duty, 16, 31, 49, 50, 51, 56, 68, 84, 89, 97, 108, 110

119

emotivism, 18-19
Epicureans, 11
Epicurus, 11 n.3
Erickson, Millard J., 73 n.7
ethical systems, 7, 8
evolutionism (evolutionary ethic), 17-18
existentialism, 16-17
evil, 11, 12, 13, 18, 45, 50, 56, 83, 96, 99, 109, 111, 113; lesser evil, 68, 70-80, 83, 96, 105, 106

first principles, 17
Fletcher, Joseph, 20-21, 70 n.5, 92-93, 110
freedom, 16-17, 19, 20, 22, 23

Gnostics, 21
God, existence of, 29-30, 32; will of, 13-14, 27, 32, 34, 51, 52, 61, 72, 76, 78, 95, 104; nature of, 13, 14, 15, 24, 25, 26, 29, 35, 52, 61, 72, 94, 95, 98, 99, 100, 104, 105; character of, 9, 23, 27, 36-38, 51, 69, 81; as moral law Giver, 31, 35, 83, 84 n.6
Golden Rule, 28
good, 11, 12, 13-14, 15, 16, 18, 46, 47, 50, 51, 54, 55, 56, 63, 71, 72, 73, 74, 75, 76, 79, 80, 96, 98, 109, 113; greater (greatest) good, 45, 68, 97

hedonism, 10, 11
Henry, Carl, 67 n.1, 69 nn. 3, 4
Heraclitus, 10
hierarchicalism, 67 n.2, 81-101, 104
Hodge, Charles, 43, 52, 60, 61, 104
humanism, 28, 29-30, 34, 35, 36, 37, 38, 39, 40
Hume, David, 29
Huxley, Julian, 17, 29-30
Huxley, T. H., 17

injustice, 19
intention (intent, motive), 44, 47, 49, 50, 55, 56, 58, 59, 60, 63, 64, 97, 109, 111; intention-act complex, 74, 110
intentionalism, 12-13

Jesus, see Christ
justice, 17, 26, 27
justification (moral), 17

Kaiser, Walter, 61, 83 n.2, 92
Kant, Immanuel, 43, 49-51, 69
Kierkegaard, Sören, 16, 84 n.6

law, 17, 34; natural, 27-31; ethical (moral), 16, 21, 23, 29, 31, 35, 39, 40-41, 50, 54, 64, 109, 110, 113; of God (divine command), 9, 13, 24, 25, 27, 30, 37, 51, 53, 59, 61, 64, 68, 69, 70, 71, 72, 73, 78, 79, 81, 83, 84, 87, 97, 98, 104, 105; civil, 90, 106, 107; hierarchy of, 24, 80, 82-101, 109; see also hierarchicalism; distinctions between, 61, 84, also n.5, 87
legalism, 64, 108, 109
Lewis, C. S., 28, 110
logos, 10
love, 26, 27, 39-40, 41, 89, 99; as absolute, 20-21, 44
Luther, Martin, 14 n.8
Lutheran tradition, 103
lying, 43, 44-65, 74, 86, 91, 92, 100, 109

meaning, 14, 19, 74
means, 16, 20-21, 49; see also results
Montgomery, John W., 70 n.5
moral conflicts (dilemmas), see conflicts, moral
moral context, 74, 110
morality, 25, 26, 28, 34, 35, 38, 39, 74
motive, see intention
Murray, John, 43, 49, 51-52, 58, 59-60

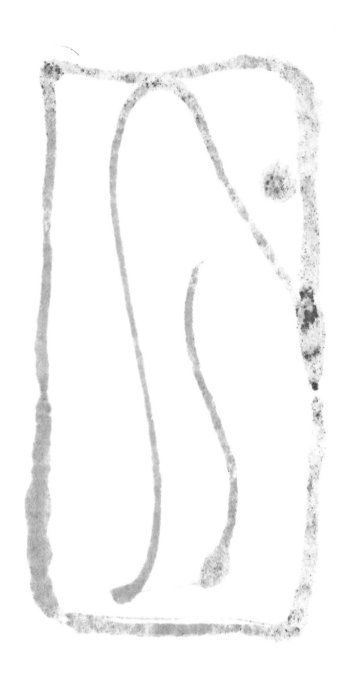

BJ1251.G43   101458
Geisler, Norm   Options in contemporary Ch

3 0094 0002 2863 2